3 Hyperlink

Student Book

Albina Escobar

Acesse o conteúdo digital em **www.pearson.com.br/hyperlink2e**
Código de acesso: **458.982.275.392**

2ª Edição – São Paulo – 2014

Pearson

Diretor editorial e de conteúdo	Roger Trimer
Gerente editorial	Kelly Tavares
Coordenadora editorial	Veronica Teodorov
Editores de desenvolvimento	Renato Malkov, João Fittipaldi
Editor de campo	Allan Cravo
Editora de mídia e desenvolvimento	Mirian Navarro
Editor assistente	Mauricio Shiroma
Editor de produção	Gustavo Reis
Assistente de arte	Lucas Medeiros
Assistente editorial	Carolina Bostigo
Editora de iconografia	Maiti Salla
Assistentes de iconografia e licenciamento de texto	Cristiane Gameiro, Rebeca Fiamozzini
Preparação de texto	Mário Vilela
Ilustração	Kleber Moraes
Criações especiais	Vendo Editorial, Estúdio Sintonia
Projeto gráfico e capa	Pedro Gentile
Editoração eletrônica	Figurattiva Editorial
Fotos da capa	GettyImages
Produção de áudio	Maximal Studio
Manual do professor	Renato Malkov, Elaine C. C. Hodgson

Créditos das imagens: p. 1 a Mangostock / Shutterstock, b Randy Faris / Corbis / Latinstock; p. 2 a Stephen Coburn / Shutterstock, b Ross Petukhov / Shutterstock; p. 3 a Tony Anderson / Corbis / Latinstock, b Ariel Skelley / Corbis / Latinstock; p. 7 www.CartoonStock.com; p. 8 a iStockphoto / Thinkstock / Getty Images, b Wavebreakmedia / Shutterstock, c Big Cheese Photo / Thinkstock / Getty Images, d John Henley / Corbis / Latinstock, e iStockphoto / Thinkstock / Getty Images, f Lifesize / Thinkstock / Getty Images; p. 9 YBob Daemmrich / Top Foto / Keystone; p. 12 a Yuri Arcurs / Shutterstock, b Yuri Arcurs / Shutterstock, c Yuri Arcurs / Shutterstock, d Edyta Pawlowska / Shutterstock, e Yuri Arcurs / Shutterstock; p. 13 iStockphoto / Thinkstock / Getty Images; p. 14 Cheryl Ravelo / Reuters / Latinstock; p. 18 Imagelab / Shutterstock; p. 20 iStockphoto / Thinkstock / Getty Images; p. 22 Igorsky / Shutterstock; p. 23 a Sergey Dolgikh / Shutterstock, b PCHT / Shutterstock; p. 24 a Donal Mullins / Shutterstock, b Anton Gvozdikov / Shutterstock, c iStockphoto / Thinkstock / Getty Images, d Gualtiero boffi / Shutterstock, e iStockphoto / Thinkstock / Getty Images, f Comstock / Thinkstock / Getty Images, g Rakov Studio / Shutterstock, h Stockbyte / Thinkstock / Getty Images, i Alena Ozerova / Shutterstock, j Digital Vision / Thinkstock / Getty Images, k Pressmaster / Shutterstock; p. 25 Armin Rose / Shutterstock; p. 26 a iStockphoto / Thinkstock / Getty Images, b Spirit of america / Shutterstock, c Kerrick James / Corbis / Latinstock; p. 27 a NASA; p. 31 iStockphoto / Thinkstock / Getty Images; p. 32 Wavebreak Media / Thinkstock / Getty Images; p. 33 a Dorling Kindersley / Thinkstock / Getty Images, b Kit Kittle / Corbis / Latinstock, c Marina Klink / LatinContent / Getty Image; p. 37 Roberto Caucino / Shutterstock; p. 38 a Patrick Poendl / Shutterstock, b Adisa / Shutterstock, c Styve Reineck / Shutterstock; p. 40 Globe Turner / Getty Images; p. 42 a Pichugin Dmitry / Shutterstock, b Phish Photography / Shutterstock, c iStockphoto / Thinkstock / Getty Images, d Gkuna / Shutterstock; p. 43 a Laurin Rinder / Shutterstock, b iStockphoto / Thinkstock / Getty Images, c iStockphoto / Thinkstock / Getty Images; p. 44 Photodisc / Thinkstock / Getty Images; p. 46 Ball David / Glow Images; p. 47 Fotosearch / Keystone; p. 49 spirit of america / Shutterstock; p. 50 a Jumbo Hostel, b Jumbo Hostel; p. 51 a Jumbo Hostel, b Jumbo Hostel, c Jumbo Hostel; p. 54 a Nordroden / Shutterstock, b Pixland / Thinkstock / Getty Images; p. 56 a AISPIX / Shutterstock, b Boris Stroujko / Shutterstock, c Dan Tautan / Shutterstock; p. 57 a iStockphoto / Thinkstock / Getty Images, b Comstock / Thinkstock / Getty Images, c iStockphoto / Thinkstock / Getty Images, d Babk Tafreshi / Getty Images, e Iakov Kalinin / Shutterstock, f S.Borisov / Shutterstock; p. 61 CreatasThinkstock / Getty Images; p. 63 a iStockphoto / Thinkstock / Getty Images, b Sarah Fields Shutterstock, c Tony Moran / Shutterstock; p. 66 Alphaspirit /Shutterstock; p. 68 The Image Works / Topfoto / Keystone; p. 71 a Denis Burdin / Shutterstock, b Pal Teravagimov / Shutterstock; p. 73 Jose Roberto Couto / Tyba; p. 74 Marcello Lourenco / Tyba; p. 75 a Jose Roberto Couto / Tyba, b Alexandre Campbell / Tyba, c Delfim Martins / Tyba; p. 80 a Lalo de Almeida / Folhapress, b Gary Yim / Shutterstock, c Vinicius Tupinamba / Shutterstock, d Nelson Antoine / Fotoarena / Folhapress, e Cleiton Thiele / Pressphoto; p. 81 a Edson Sato / Pulsar Imagens, b Maridav / Shutterstock, c Yuri Arcurs / Shutterstock, d Lidara / Shutterstock, e Santhosh Kumar / Shutterstock, f BananaStock / Thinkstock / Getty Images, g Photos.com / Thinkstock / Getty Images, h iStockphoto / Thinkstock / Getty Images, i iStockphoto / Thinkstock / Getty Images, j Photodisc / Thinkstock / Getty Images; p. 85 a Val Thoermer / Shutterstoc, b Gabriel Boieras / SambaPhoto; p. 87 a Ormuzd Alves / Folhapress, b Christian Tragni / Folhapress, c Paul Brighton / Shutterstock; p. 96 iStockphoto / Thinkstock / Getty Images

Dados Internacionais de Catalogação na Publicação (CIP)
(Câmara Brasileira do Livro, SP, Brasil)

Escobar, Albina
Hyperlink : student book, 3 / Albina Escobar. --
2. ed. -- São Paulo : Pearson Education do Brasil, 2014.
ISBN 978-85-8143-902-0
1. Inglês (Ensino médio) I. Título.

13-07793 CDD-420.7

Índices para catálogo sistemático:
1. Inglês : Ensino médio 420.7

ISBN 978-85-8143-902-0 Hyperlink 3 Student Book - 2a ed
ISBN 978-85-430-0046-6 Hyperlink 3 Student Book with eText - 2a ed
ISBN 978-85-8143-919-8 Hyperlink 3 Student Book with MyEnglishLab - 2a ed
ISBN 978-85-8143-910-5 Hyperlink 3 Teacher Book - 2a ed

Pearson Education do Brasil Ltda.,
uma empresa do grupo Pearson Education
Rua Nélson Francisco, 26 – CEP: 02712-100 – São Paulo, SP – Brasil

10 9 8 7 6 5 4 3 outubro/2015

Caro aluno,

A língua inglesa é um conhecimento que não se encerra em si mesmo, mas abre portas para novas descobertas. O livro que tem em mãos irá ajudá-lo nesse processo de descobertas. Observe como aproveitar seu livro ao máximo.

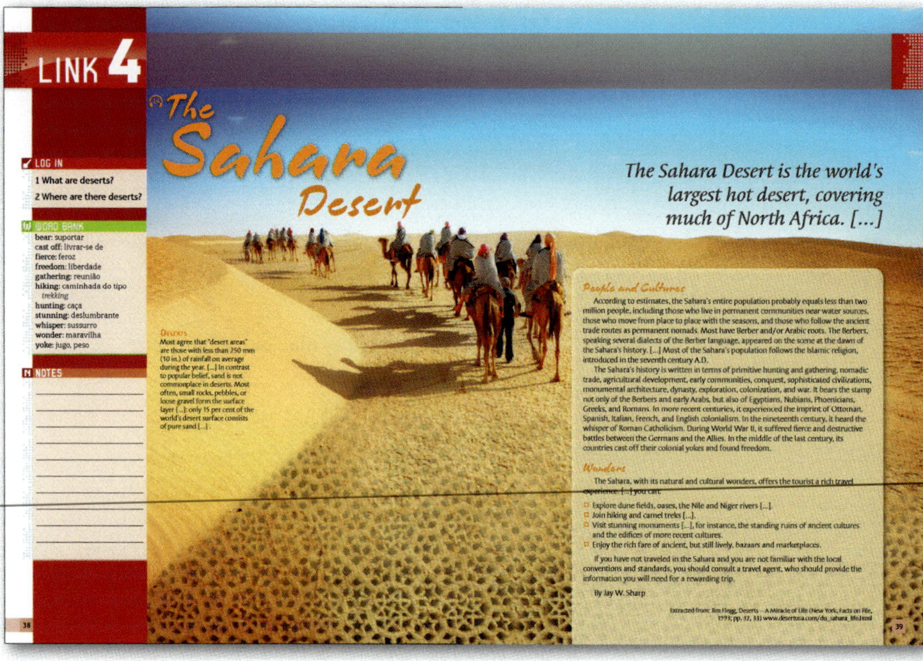

TEXT

Cada unidade é iniciada com um texto sobre temas atuais e diversos. O **Log In** levanta questões para você considerar e discutir antes da leitura e o **Word Bank** apresenta palavras cruciais para a compreensão de cada texto.

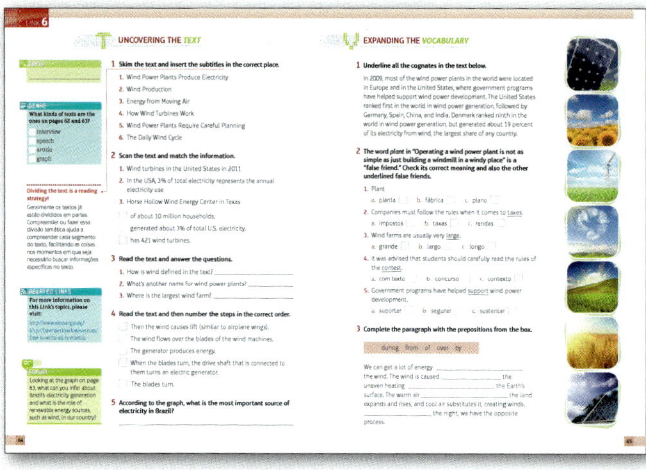

EXPANDING THE VOCABULARY

Essa seção oferece uma oportunidade para que você aumente seu vocabulário, analisando e trabalhando com as palavras apresentadas no texto.

UNCOVERING THE TEXT

Aqui você aprofunda seu entendimento do texto, explorando diferentes gêneros e respondendo a perguntas de compreensão e interpretação. Você também encontra aqui links para websites que se aprofundam nos temas explorados.

DISCOVERING GRAMMAR

Um atalho para a mecânica da língua inglesa é o que você encontra aqui. A cada unidade você tem a chance de explorar tópicos gramaticais, desenvolvendo o domínio formal do inglês.

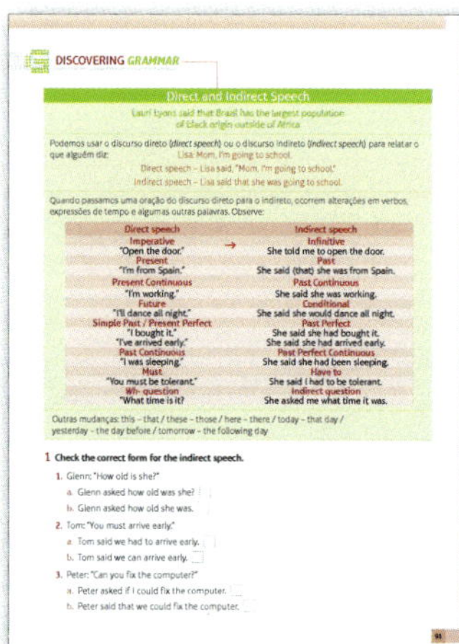

COMMUNICATION BYTES

O foco dessa seção é a comunicação oral genuína sobre assuntos relevantes. Aqui você se prepara para expressar suas próprias ideias e opiniões, explorando modelos e informações necessárias para o desenvolvimento de diálogos.

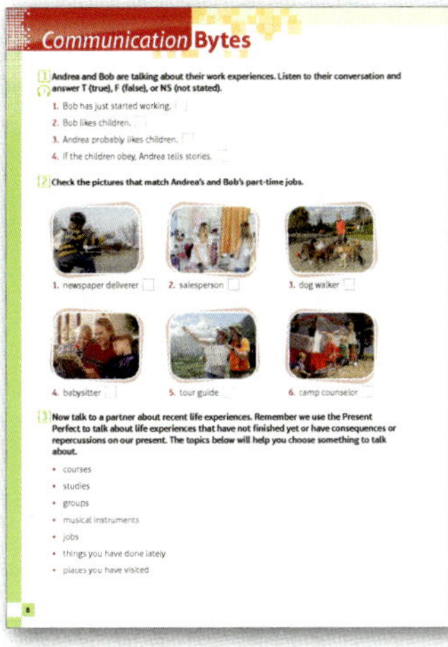

WRITING BITS

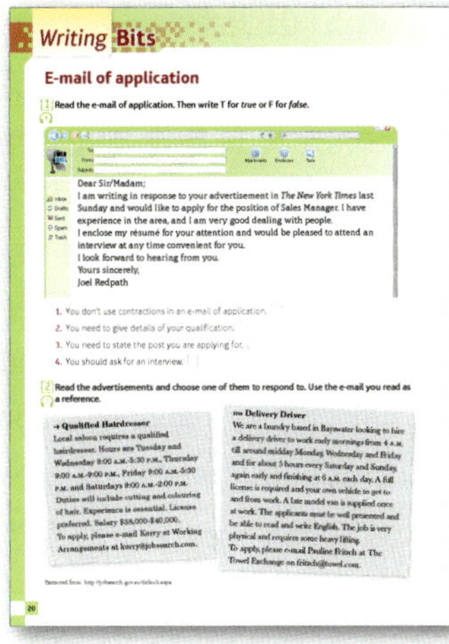

A produção escrita é o tema central aqui. Cada unidade lhe apresenta uma proposta de criação de texto, explorando gêneros variados e oferecendo modelos de diferentes estruturas textuais.

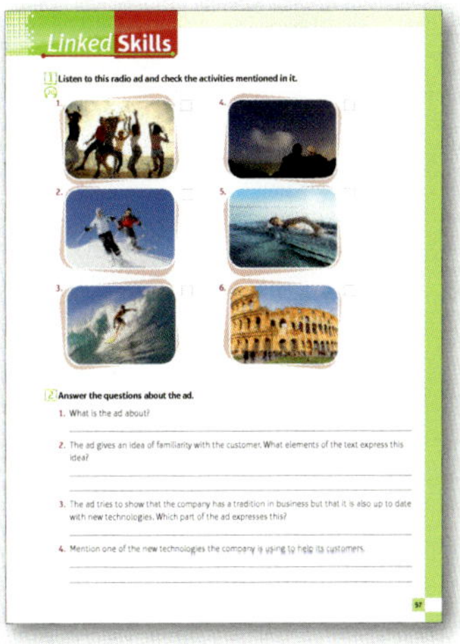

LINKED SKILLS

Aqui combinamos a habilidade de escuta com as outras aptidões. Você encontra nessa seção uma chance de conectar o texto falado ao escrito, ouvindo inglês falado com fluência e respondendo (de forma oral e escrita) às ideias apresentadas.

REVIEW

Para checar seu entendimento, e para que o conteúdo estudado seja ainda melhor fixado, a cada duas unidades você encontra uma revisão, com exercícios que retomam os tópicos explorados.

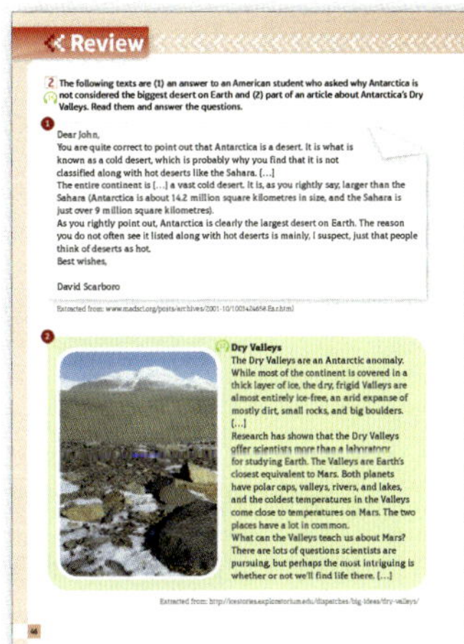

WORLD LINKS

Expandir as temáticas propostas pelos textos presentes em cada unidade é a proposta dessa seção. Você é convidado a repensar sua posição em relação ao mundo atual e as relações que nele desenvolvemos.

SO FAR, SO GOOD?

Aqui você reflete sobre seu aprendizado, baseado na análise pessoal do seu desempenho.

Primeiro você participa de uma atividade lúdica, depois avalia o próprio entendimento dos temas trabalhados.

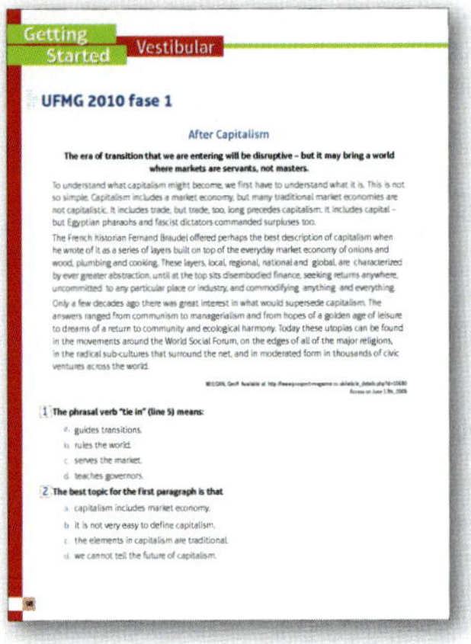

GETTING STARTED: VESTIBULAR

A possibilidade de aplicar seu conhecimento a questões extraídas de provas de vestibular é o que se apresenta nessa seção. Aqui você pode testar seu domínio da língua inglesa e familiarizar-se com o conteúdo avaliado em vestibulares de renomadas universidades.

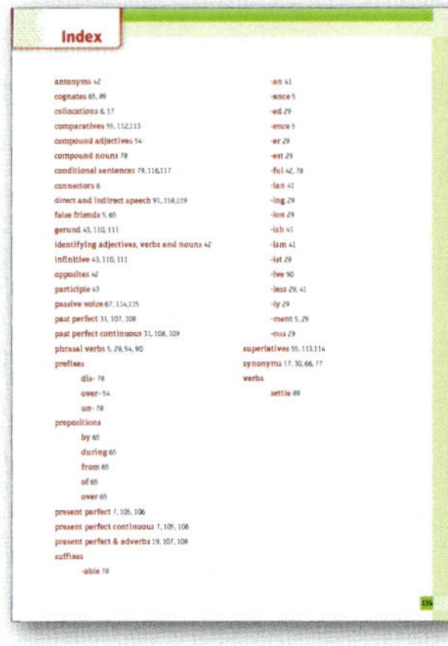

INDEX

Aqui você encontra tópicos gramaticais e de vocabulário organizados de maneira compilada.

GRAMMAR

Essa seção oferece a possibilidade de praticar mais a fundo os tópicos gramaticais apresentados no livro, resolvendo exercícios focados nos referidos tópicos.

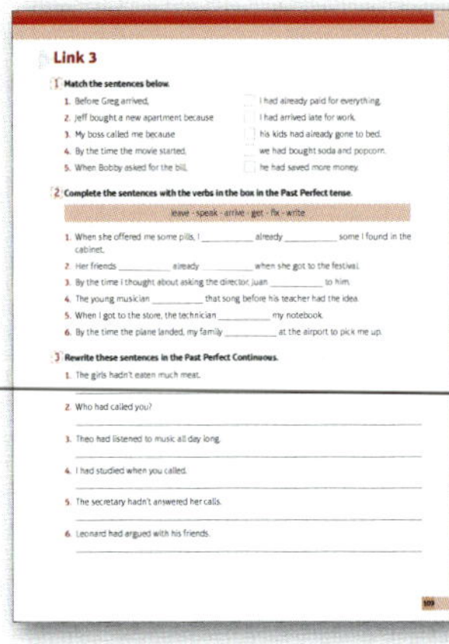

VOCABULARY LOG

Esse espaço é destinado à criação de um glossário pessoal, com vocabulário que você julgue importante.

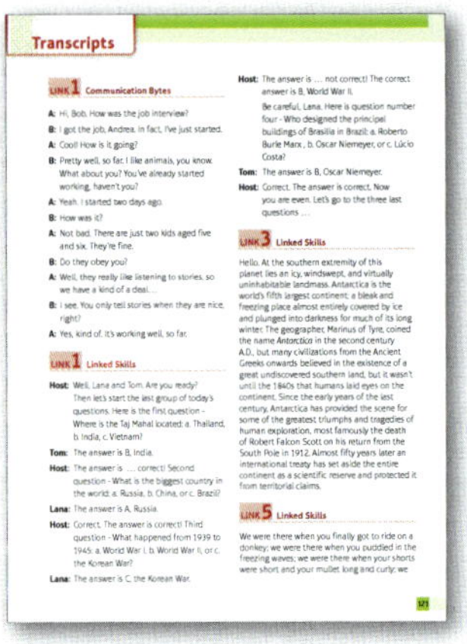

TRANSCRIPTS

Você pode consultar aqui as transcrições dos textos de áudio apresentados no livro.

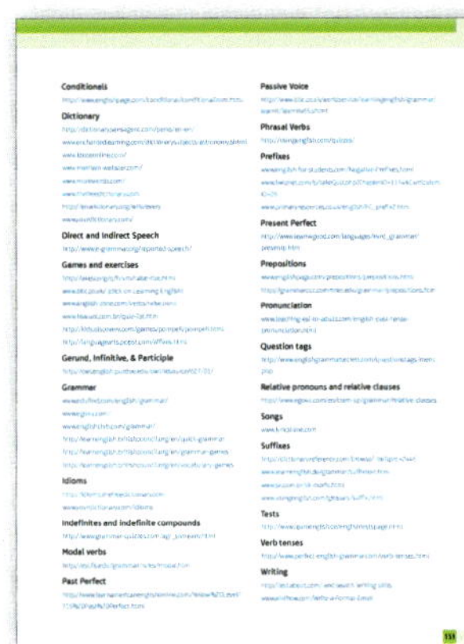

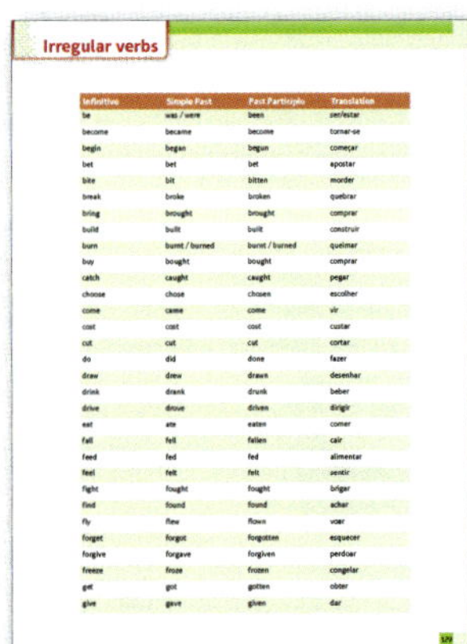

GLOSSARY

Aqui você encontra palavras presentes no livro que podem ser desconhecidas.

IRREGULAR VERBS

Encontre aqui uma lista de verbos irregulares para sua referência.

REFERENCES

Essa seção oferece oportunidades para que você explore vídeos, websites e outros livros que expandem os temas trabalhados nas unidades apresentadas aqui.

Hyperlinks

teenagers + jobs

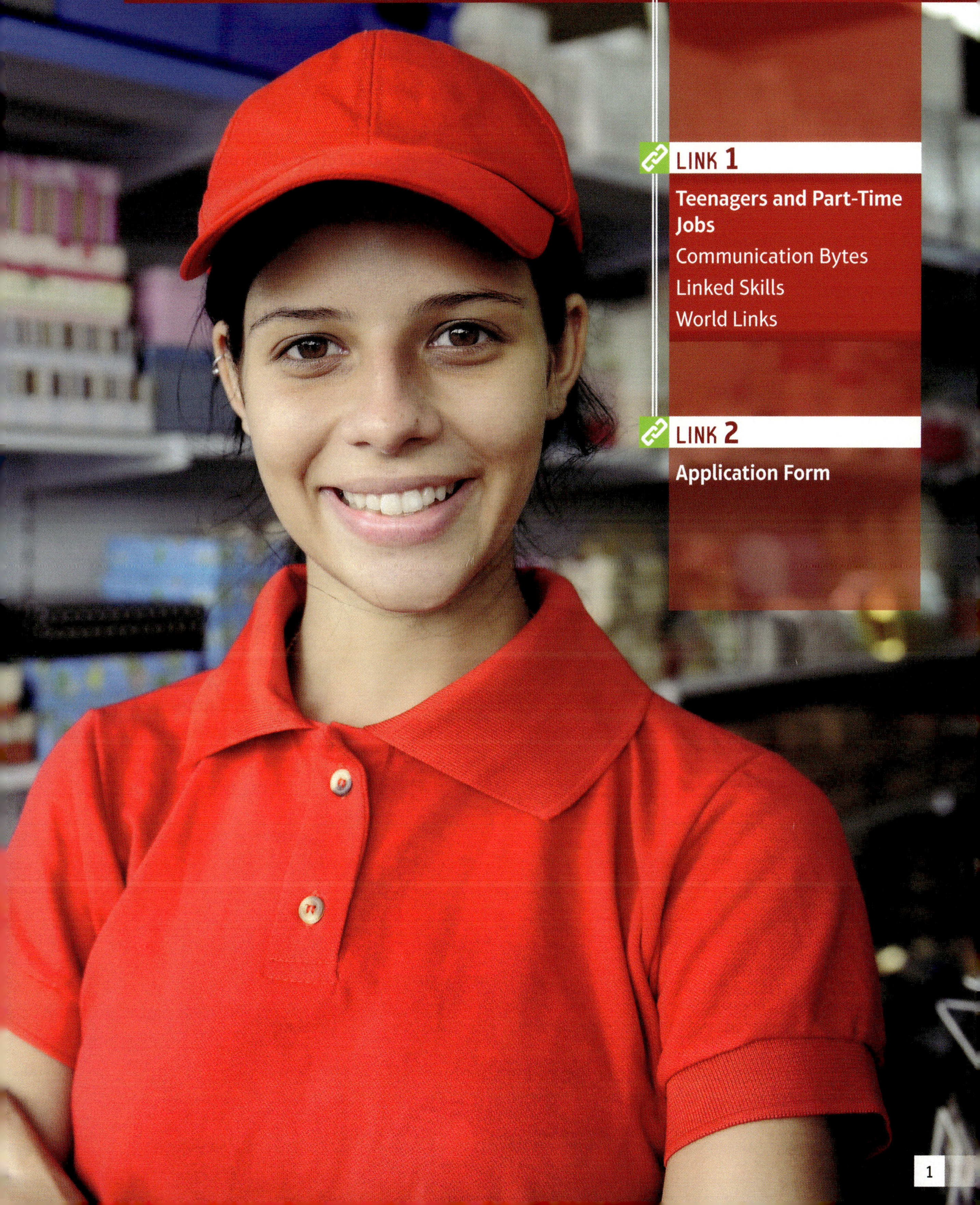

LINK 1

Teenagers and Part-Time Jobs

Communication Bytes

Linked Skills

World Links

LINK 2

Application Form

LINK 1

LOG IN

1 Take a look at the text pages. What is it about?

2 Do teenagers usually work in Brazil? Why? Why not?

WORD BANK

achieve: adquirir
adulthood: vida adulta
carefree: despreocupado
develop: desenvolver
employment: emprego
goal: objetivo
hold: possuir
labor: trabalho
nearly: quase, aproximadamente
praise: elogiar
set: estabelecer
youth: juventude

NOTES

2

Adolescence is that difficult period of time when carefree children transition to responsible adults... we hope. That is the goal, after all, for teens to develop into mature, productive, responsible members of the community. One method for assisting this transition is obtaining part-time employment. A job can help teenagers better develop their identities, obtain increased autonomy, achieve new accomplishments, develop work experience, and become more independent from their parents.

According to the U.S. Department of Labor, 50 percent of American teenagers hold informal jobs, such as babysitting or yard work, by age 12. Boys tend to begin their jobs at younger ages and work more hours than girls. By age 15, nearly two-thirds of American teens have had some kind of employment. By the time teens graduate from high school, 80% will have held a part-time job at some time during the school year. [...]

Researchers have studied and debated the benefits and drawbacks of teens and part-time jobs for more than 2 decades. Many researchers, including those on government panels like the National Commission on Youth, praise part-time work and say it contributes to the transition from youth to adulthood. Other studies have found significant negative consequences to students working over 20 hours a week. [...]

Summer employment is an excellent alternative, as it does not interfere with schooling and provides teens with a constructive use of their free time. [...]

The U.S. Department of Labor sets the minimum age for employment at 14. It also limits the number of hours worked by minors under the age of 16. However, minimum age requirements do not apply to minors employed by their parents or guardian. [...]

Extracted from: http://middleearthnj.wordpress.com/2010/04/02/teenagers-and-part-time-jobs-benefits-drawbacks-and-tips/

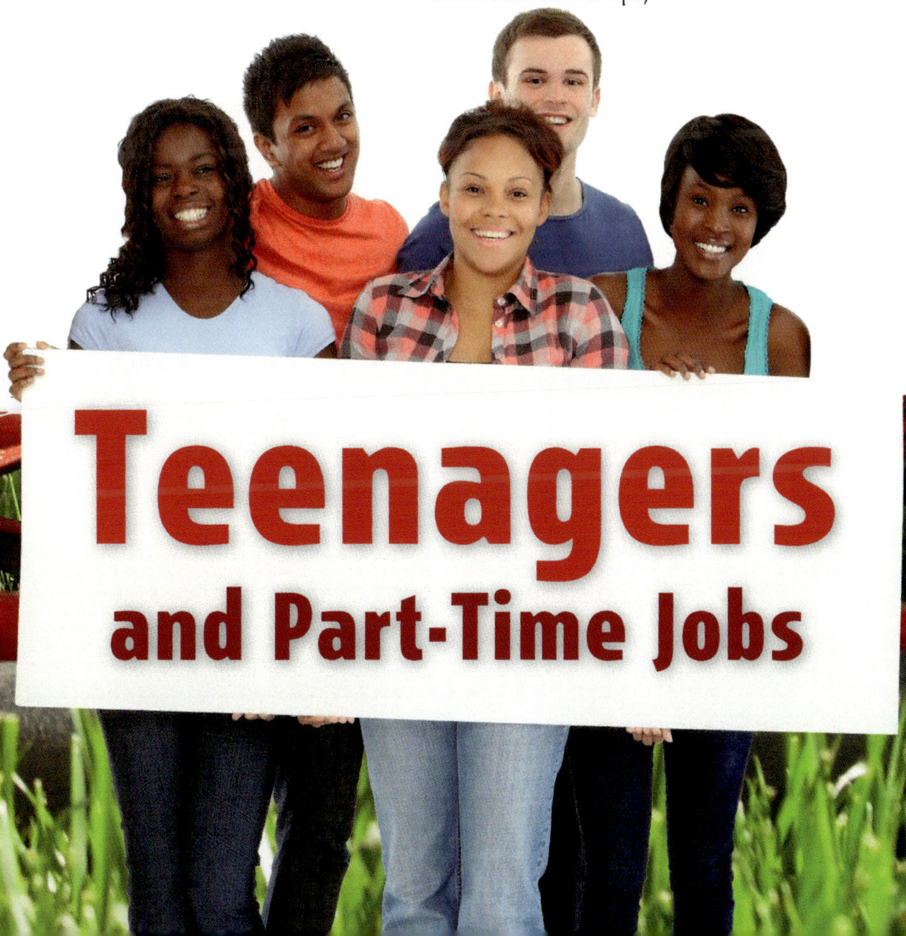

Teenagers and Part-Time Jobs

UNCOVERING THE *TEXT*

TOPIC

____

GENRE

What kind of text is on pages 2 and 3?

- [ ] a form
- [ ] an article
- [ ] a book review
- [ ] a survey

Talking about the subject is a reading strategy!

Conversar sobre o assunto a ser lido é uma estratégia de leitura. Vai ajudar você a colher informações sobre o assunto e a compreender melhor o texto.

RELATED LINKS

For more information on this Link's topics, please visit:

http://www.quintcareers.com/teen_jobs.html

http://www.cnn.com/2011/09/16/living/workplace-professional-dress-cb

FORUM

In the USA, Canada, Europe, and many other countries around the world, teenagers are allowed to do some kinds of work. What is acceptable regarding teenagers working in Brazil?

1 What do you think about the statement below? Talk to a friend about it. In the USA, teens work to buy their things, to have money for expenses (car, recreation, clothing), to save money for college, or to help their families.

2 Scan the text and complete the information.

The number of teens that...

1. have held some informal job by age twelve: ________
2. have held some employment by age fifteen: ________
3. have held some part-time job by graduation time: ________

3 Check the alternatives that are *not* correct according to the text.

1. Part-time employment...
   a. may help teens gain autonomy. [ ]
   b. takes teens away from their families. [ ]
   c. helps teens develop identity. [ ]
   d. may turn teens against the community. [ ]
2. According to some researchers,...
   a. part-time jobs offer no benefits or drawbacks to teens. [ ]
   b. part-time jobs contribute to the transition from youth to adulthood. [ ]
   c. the government should offer part-time jobs to students. [ ]
   d. teens should have part-time employment in government jobs. [ ]

4 Answer the questions.

1. Why is summer employment an alternative?

   ____

2. In your opinion, what may be the negative consequences to students working over twenty hours a week? (Answer in English or in Portuguese.)

   ____

   ____

EXPANDING THE *VOCABULARY*

1 Match the underlined words to their correct translation according to the text.

1. A job can help teenagers obtain <u>increased</u> autonomy.
2. They can also achieve new <u>accomplishments</u>.
3. Researchers have studied the benefits and <u>drawbacks</u> of teens and part-time jobs.
4. By age fifteen, <u>nearly</u> two-thirds of American teens have had some kind of employment.

☐ realizações
☐ desvantagens
☐ quase
☐ aumentado(a)

2 Find the false friends.

adolescence – period – transition – parents – responsible
identity – autonomy – obtain – experience

____

False Friends

Cognatos são palavras com a mesma origem e significado. Quando diferem no significado, são chamadas "falsos cognatos", "falsos amigos" ou, mais propriamente, cognatos de sentido diferente.

3 In "That is the goal, after all, for teens to develop into mature, productive, responsible members of the community," *develop into* is a phrasal verb. Match the best meaning to the underlined phrasal verbs.

1. <u>Hold on</u>; Alex will answer the phone in a minute.
   a. hold firmly ☐ b. wait for a short period of time ☐
2. Ten men wearing masks <u>held</u> the bank <u>up</u> this morning.
   a. rob ☐ b. hide ☐
3. She <u>held back</u> her tears at her daughter's wedding.
   a. hide ☐ b. show ☐
4. Our plan <u>worked out</u> fine.
   a. exercise ☐ b. be successful ☐

Phrasal Verb

É formado de um verbo mais uma partícula que modifica o significado desse verbo.
Ex.: *hold* = possuir; *hold on* = esperar; *hold up* = assaltar; *hold back* = conter.

4 In the text, we see the word *employment* used several times. It is a noun created when we add the suffix *-ment* to the verb *employ*. Add *-ance*, *-ence*, or *-ment* to create other nouns.

1. inherit: ______________________
2. reside: ______________________
3. perform: ______________________
4. nourish: ______________________

Suffixes

Os sufixos *-ment*, *-ance* e *-ence* (= a ação de; o resultado da ação de) podem formar substantivos. Ex.:
arrange – *arrange***ment**;
resist – *resist***ance**;
refer – *refer***ence**.

5 **Choose the best connector to complete the sentences.**

however – although – such as – like – but

1. Jobs __________ gardening can be held part-time.
2. He was quite ill. __________, he didn't go to the doctor.
3. I want to go out, __________ I haven't done the dishes.
4. Juice, __________ milk, is good for our health.
5. __________ they had not studied, they all passed the exams.

Connectors

São palavras ou locuções usadas para ligar outras palavras ou frases. Ex.: *and* (e), *but* (mas), *when* (quando), *after* (após), *however* (entretanto), *such as* (tal como), *like* (como), *although* (embora) etc.

6 **Read the comic strip and the paragraph to answer the next questions.**

How social media can affect your job search.

by Laura Vander Kam, Real Simple

[...]"Your first impression isn't made with a firm handshake—it's with a Google search," says Dan Schawbel, the author of "Me 2.0."

A recent survey confirms this: A whopping 70 percent of U.S. business managers say they decided not to hire a job candidate based upon something found out about her online.

So it's crucial to keep your virtual self, well, virtuous. [...]

Extracted from: http://www.cnn.com/2012/10/09/living/real-simple-social-media-job

1. What does the employer mean when he says, "There's no way you're getting this job"?
   a. The person will get the job for sure. ☐
   b. There are no possibilities that the person will get the job. ☐
2. What is the meaning of the sentence "It's a bit stalkery, perhaps, to look at what is publicly available on social networks of a candidate you are trying to assess, but completely legal"?
   a. Employers can check their employees' Facebook profile to see if they are working or not. ☐
   b. Although it is a bit weird, there are no legal prohibitions for an employer to check the Facebook profile of a person he's/she's thinking about hiring to help him/her make this decision. ☐

Collocations

Na tirinha temos a *collocation get a job*. Veja outros exemplos com *get*: *get a shock, get angry, get divorced, get drunk, get frightened, get home, get lost, get married, get nowhere, get permission, get pregnant, get ready, get started.*

DISCOVERING GRAMMAR

Present Perfect

By age 15, nearly two-thirds of American teens *have had* some kind of employment.
Other studies *have found* significant negative consequences to students working over 20 hours a week.

O *Present Perfect* é usado para expressar ações que tiveram seu início no passado, mas que ainda não se encerraram; ou quando não há necessidade de especificar o tempo, focando unicamente na ação. Por exemplo:

Quando falamos sobre experiências de vida:

I *have traveled* to many different places in Brazil. / They *have not visited* their grandparents in France.

Quando falamos sobre mudanças que acontecem num período indeterminado de tempo:

They *have made* the tests more difficult. / *Has* it *changed* a lot?

Quando falamos sobre conquistas: Men *has walked* on the Moon. / She *hasn't received* any awards.

Quando falamos sobre ações que perduram:

We *have won* six of the seven matches. / Where *have* you *worked* for the last few years?

Ao construirmos frases com o *Present Perfect*, utilizamos o verbo auxiliar *have* e o verbo principal em seu *Past Participle*. O *Past Participle* de verbos regulares é o mesmo que o seu *Simple Past*, mas com muitos verbos irregulares o *Past Participle* é diferente do *Simple Past*. Confira a tabela de verbos irregulares para tirar possíveis dúvidas.

Estrutura:

Frases afirmativas: sujeito + *have* + *Past Participle* do verbo principal + complemento

Frases interrogativas: *have* + sujeito + *Past Participle* do verbo principal + complemento

Frases negativas: sujeito + *have* + not + *Past Participle* do verbo principal + complemento

Note: Assim como no *Present Perfect*, o *Present Perfect Continuous* expressa ações que tiveram seu início no passado e ainda não terminaram, entretanto, a estrutura dá a entender que é uma situação temporária, que tem um fim previsto.

have + been + verbo+ing: I *have been working* hard.

1 Complete the sentences with the Present Perfect tense.

1. She ____________________ (see) that movie many times.
2. The tourists ____________________ (spend) all their money.
3. The girls ____________________ (go) out with their friends.
4. The Scientists ____________________ (discover) a new drug.
5. Nobody ____________________ (leave). They are all in here.
6. The children ____________________ (arrive) home.
7. Gina and Karin ____________________ (do) their homework.
8. The show ____________________ (be) on for half an hour.

Communication Bytes

1 **Andrea and Bob are talking about their work experiences. Listen to their conversation and answer T (true), F (false), or NS (not stated).**

3

1. Bob has just started working. ☐
2. Bob likes children. ☐
3. Andrea probably likes children. ☐
4. If the children obey, Andrea tells stories. ☐

2 **Check the pictures that match Andrea's and Bob's part-time jobs.**

1. newspaper deliverer ☐

2. salesperson ☐

3. dog walker ☐

4. babysitter ☐

5. tour guide ☐

6. camp counselor ☐

3 **Now talk to a partner about recent life experiences. Remember we use the Present Perfect to talk about life experiences that have not finished yet or have consequences or repercussions on our present. The topics below will help you choose something to talk about.**

- courses
- studies
- groups
- musical instruments
- jobs
- things you have done lately
- places you have visited

Linked Skills

1 Another area teenagers can work in is show business. Can you think of some famous teenage actors, actresses, or singers?

____

____

2 Television game shows are very common, and even if you are not famous, it's an opportunity to be on TV. Listen to a game show and choose the title that fits this show best. Justify your answer.

1. High School Quiz Show ☐
2. Pets Win Prizes ☐
3. Blind Date ☐

____

____

____

3 Tom and Lana are tied. Write the three last questions they will have to answer.

____

____

____

4 Now, share the questions you created with your friends and see if they know the answers.

What your clothes say about you

1

- In an interview your attire plays a supporting role.

[...]

- Appropriate attire supports your image as a person who takes the interview process seriously and understands the nature of the industry in which you are trying to become employed.
- Be aware that in some industries, customer contact and image presented to the customer is critical. In such industries, your attire will be judged more critically.
- Your attire should be noticed as being appropriate and well-fitting, but it should not take center stage.

[...]

- Even if you are aware that employees of an organization dress casually on the job, dress more formally for the interview unless you are specifically told otherwise by the employer. The interview is a professional meeting and thus a more formal occasion than daily work.
- Never confuse an interview or business function with a social event. Don't dress for a party or a date. [...]

INTERVIEW ATTIRE GUIDELINES FOR MEN AND WOMEN

2

SUIT:

- A two-piece matched suit is always the best and safest choice.

What if the JOB is in a NON-SUIT-wearing WORK ENVIRONMENT:

3 • Even if you would or could wear jeans on the job, or the work environment is outdoors and a very non-suit environment, wearing a suit to the interview shows you take the interview seriously as a professional meeting. Dressing well is a compliment to the person(s) with whom you meet. If you think the industry in which you're interviewing would frown on a suit, or the interview will involve going to a work site where a suit would be inappropriate, look for advice through professional organizations, your professors who have been employed in that industry, and/or by asking the employer directly and politely. One alternative is to wear pressed pants (like khakis) and a dark jacket; less formal than a suit, but still business-appropriate for both men and women. [...]

4 **DETAILS:**

- Everything should be clean and well pressed.
- Carefully inspect clothes for tags, dangling threads, etc. [...]

5 **HAIR:**

- Should be clean and neat. [...]

HANDS:

- Clean fingernails [...]

6 **SMELL:**

- Perfume or cologne should be used sparingly or not at all. Remember that some people have allergies/sensitivities; you'd hate for that to derail an interview. No odors in clothes. [...]

Extracted from: http://www.career.vt.edu/interviewing/interviewappearance.html

World links

Reading Comprehension

1 Check the looks which are *not* suitable for job interviews according to the text.

1

2

3

4

5

2 By reading the text it's possible to infer that , besides clothing, general look is also important in a job interview. Mention a part of the text that supports this.

3 In movies, a supporting role is played by someone who is close to the main character. What does it mean to say, "In an interview, your attire plays a supporting role"? Answer in Portuguese.

4 What information can't be found in the text?

1. What type of clothes to wear for a job interview. ☐
2. What to say during an interview. ☐
3. What kind of shoes to wear for the interview. ☐

Hyperlinks

teenagers + jobs

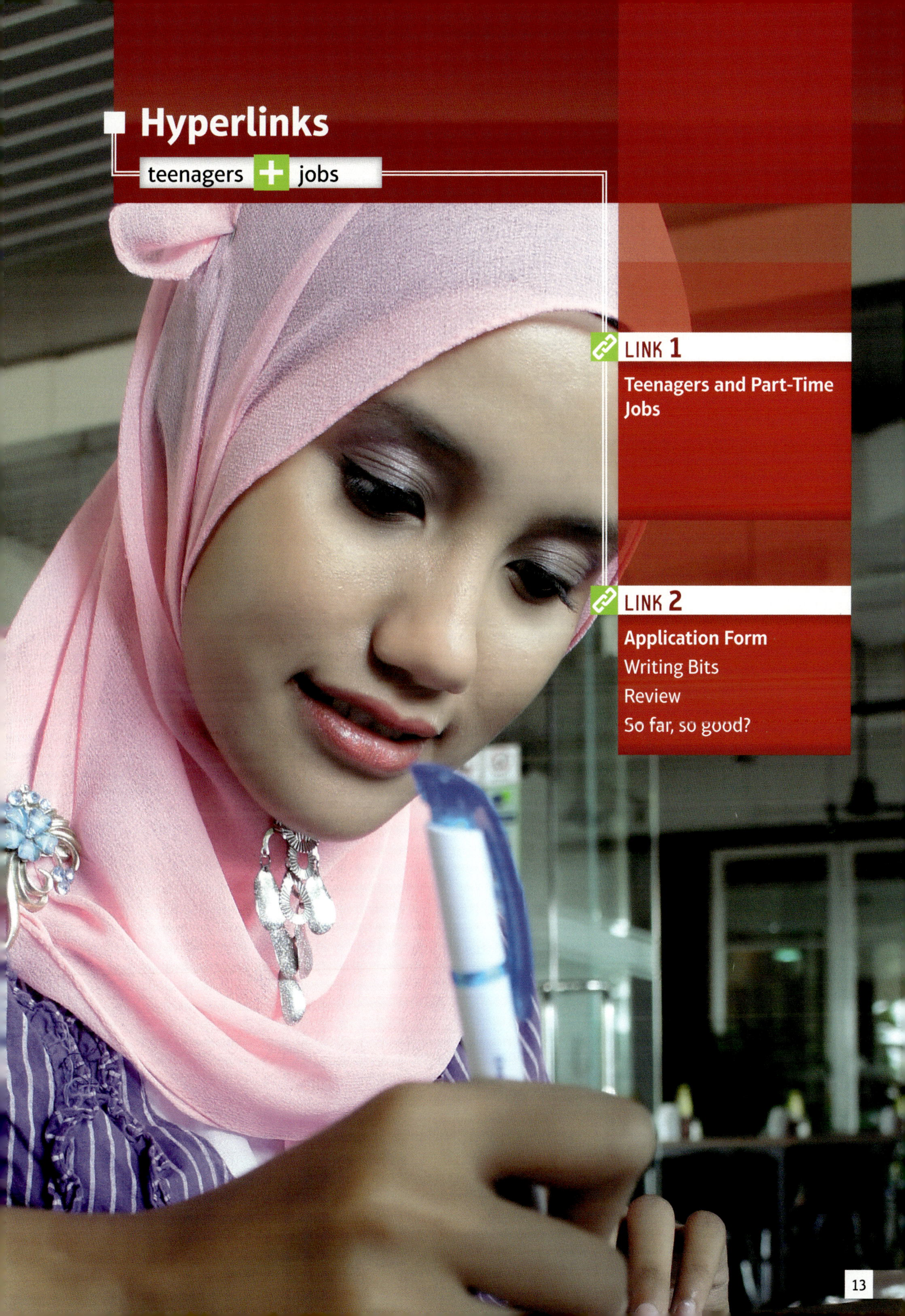

LINK 2

LOG IN

1 In your opinion, how do companies select their employees?

2 Have you ever filled in an application form?

WORD BANK

advancement: avanço
application form: formulário
apply for: candidatar-se
attach: anexar
available: disponível
background: experiência
degree: graduação (diploma de curso superior)
duty: obrigação
provide: fornecer

NOTES

SAMPLE EMPLOYMENT APPLICATION FORM

Date: / /

Name: Last First Middle Maiden

Address: Number Street City State Zip

Telephone: ( )

If under 18, please list age:

Position applied for (1):

and salary desired (2):
(be specific)

DAYS/HOURS AVAILABLE TO WORK

No Pref Mon Tue Wed
Thur Fr Sat Sun

How many hours can you work weekly?

Can you work nights?

Employment desired
- full-time only
- part-time only
- full or part-time

When available for work?

Type of school	Name of school	Location (complete mailing address)	Number of years completed	Major & degree
High school				
College				

An application form sometimes makes it difficult for an individual to adequately summarize a complete background. Use the space below to summarize any additional information necessary to describe your full qualifications for the specific position for which you are applying.

MILITARY

Have you ever been in the armed forces? ☐ Yes ☐ No

WORK EXPERIENCE

Please list your work experience for the past five years beginning with your most recent job held. If you were self-employed, give firm name. Attach additional sheets if necessary.

Name of employer:

Address:

City, State, Zip Code:

Phone number:

Name of last supervisor:

Employment dates

From: / / To: / /

Pay or salary

Start: Final:

Your last job title

Reason for leaving (be specific)

List the jobs you held, duties performed, skills used or learned, advancements or promotions while you worked at this company.

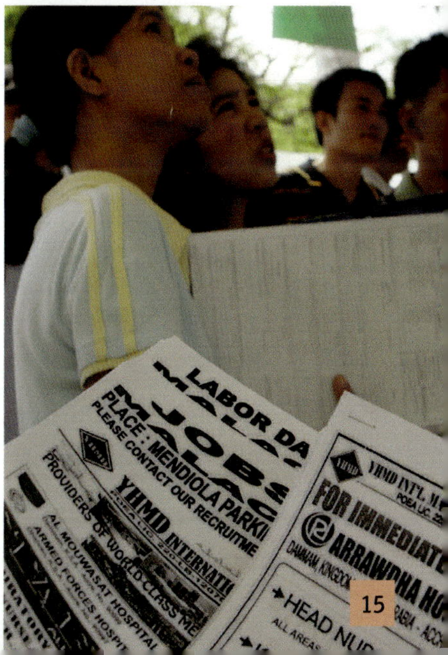

May we contact your present employer? ☐ No ☐ Yes

Extracted from: www.entrepreneur.com/formnet/form/1023

UNCOVERING THE *TEXT*

TOPIC

____

GENRE

What kind of text is on pages 14 and 15?

- ☐ a form
- ☐ an interview
- ☐ instructions
- ☐ a survey

Scanning is a reading strategy!

Passar os olhos pelo texto de forma detalhada em busca de informações específicas ajuda-nos a encontrar caminhos para compreender o texto.

RELATED LINKS

For more information on this Link's topics, please visit:

http://www.career.vt.edu/job-searchguide/email.html

http://www.picturecorrect.com/tips/high-speed-photography/

FORUM

How important is having work experience before entering college?

1 **Scan the text and check the types of information you are being required to provide.**

1. personal information ☐
2. position desired ☐
3. education, and background information ☐
4. family information ☐
5. work experience ☐
6. hobbies, preferences ☐
7. military ☐

2 **Match the words to their meaning.**

1. A part-time job is
2. A temporary job is
3. A regular job is
4. Employment is
5. A full-time job is
6. Self-employed are

☐ one that doesn't have a specific time to end.

☐ one that lasts only for a definite period of time.

☐ regular job that requires less than forty hours of work during a week.

☐ work, especially when done to earn money.

☐ a job that usually involves forty hours of work during a week.

☐ people who work for themselves.

3 **Classify the statements as T for *true*, F for *false*, or NS for *not stated* according to the form.**

1. The company is looking for drivers. ☐
2. The company won't accept people who have been convicted of crimes. ☐
3. It is necessary to have a car to get the job. ☐
4. The company may want to contact the present employer. ☐
5. The applicant must have been in the armed forces. ☐
6. The present employer has to be contacted. ☐

EXPANDING THE *VOCABULARY*

1 **Complete the sentences with the words from the box to form collocations.**

> **Collocations**
>
> São palavras geralmente usadas em conjunto. Ex.: *temporary job, full-time job, part-time job, a well-paid job.*

volunteer   out of   overtime   permit   part-time

1. My father stays in his office until very late. He usually works *overtime*.
2. I am going to join an NGO and do some ____________ work.
3. If you want to get a job in the USA, you need to get a work ____________.
4. Sarah was fired. She's been ____________ work for three weeks now.
5. I can't work all day long. I need a ____________ job.

2 **Scan the application form and find words with similar meanings.**

1. job: ____________
2. solely : ____________
3. inflict: ____________
4. violation: ____________
5. business: ____________

3 **Check the correct meaning of the underlined words.**

1. Are you <u>currently</u> employed?
   a. often ☐   b. at the moment ☐   c. usually ☐
2. He helped her <u>only</u> for love.
   a. exactly ☐   b. frequently ☐   c. exclusively ☐
3. I permit the company to examine the information I have <u>provided</u>.
   a. furnish ☐   b. take ☐   c. lend ☐
4. I'm sure I <u>suit</u> the company. I'm the right person for the job.
   a. be acceptable ☐   b. disagree ☐   c. understand ☐

4 Match the words from the box to the definitions.

offend	offense	offending	offensively	offender

1. ______________: causing someone to feel annoyed or upset
2. ______________: a transgression of law, a crime
3. ______________: in an offensive manner
4. ______________: to cause displeasure, anger, resentment
5. ______________: a person responsible for wrongdoing

5 Check the correct alternative to complete the sentences.

1. I had to fill out three __________ forms for that position.
   a. apply ☐ b. applicants ☐ c. application ☐
2. She wants to __________ for a summer job.
   a. apply ☐ b. applicants ☐ c. application ☐
3. My father's company has more than 450 __________.
   a. employ ☐ b. employment ☐ c. employees ☐
4. I have some __________ of computer science.
   a. know ☐ b. knowing ☐ c. knowledge ☐
5. This information is really __________ to the recruiting process.
   a. relevant ☐ b. relevance ☐ c. relevantly ☐

6 Fill in the blanks with the words from the box.

available	qualifications	fired	opportunities

WEB MAIL

To:
From:
Subject:

Attachments Emoticons Tools

Inbox
Drafts
Sent
Spam
Trash

Dear Marcus,

How are you? I am writing because Jonathan was ______________ last week. He is looking for a job, and I thought maybe you could help. He is ______________ to start working immediately, and he has a lot of ______________. Please, let us know if you hear of any good ______________.

Best wishes,

Lena

DISCOVERING GRAMMAR

Present Perfect & Adverbs

Have you ever been in the armed forces?

Adverbs	Examples
1. **since** / **for**	I have worked here **since** May. / I have worked here **for** two months.
(desde / por, durante)	*Trabalho aqui desde maio. / Trabalho aqui há dois meses.*
2. **ever** / **never**	Have you **ever** seen a dolphin? / I have **never** seen a dolphin.
(alguma vez / nunca)	*Você já viu um golfinho? / Nunca vi um golfinho.*
3. **already**	Has he **already** left? / He has **already** left.
(já)	*Ele já saiu? / Ele já saiu.*
4. **yet**	Has she arrived **yet**? / She hasn't arrived **yet**.
(já, ainda)	*Ela já chegou? / Ela ainda não chegou.*
5. **just**	We have **just** met the director.
(acabou de acontecer)	*Acabamos de encontrar/conhecer o diretor.*
6. **recently** / **lately**	Have you seen Tom **recently** / **lately**?
(recentemente, ultimamente)	*Você tem visto Tom recentemente / ultimamente?*
7. **many times**	We've been to the zoo **many times**.
(muitas vezes)	*Fomos ao zoológico muitas vezes.*

Os advérbios associados ao *Present Perfect* não definem um período de tempo. Como o *Simple Past* é usado para expressar uma ação passada finalizada e ocorrida num momento específico, usamos outros tipos de advérbio ou de expressão temporal: *I graduated in 2012*; *We had some ice cream yesterday*.

1 Check the correct answer to fill in the blanks.

1. ______________ to England?
   a. Did you ever been ☐ b. Have you be ☐ c. Have you ever been ☐
2. That's the most difficult exercise I ______________.
   a. did ☐ b. ever do ☐ c. have ever done ☐
3. It's clear that you ______________ this book yet.
   a. haven't read ☐ b. do read ☐ c. don't read ☐
4. My mother ______________ my aunt last night.
   a. phoned ☐ b. has phoned ☐ c. didn't phoned ☐
5. I ______________ all my exams last term.
   a. did passed ☐ b. passed ☐ c. have passed ☐

E-mail of application

1 **Read the e-mail of application. Then write T for *true* or F for *false*.**

Dear Sir/Madam;

I am writing in response to your advertisement in *The New York Times* last Sunday and would like to apply for the position of Sales Manager. I have experience in the area, and I am very good dealing with people.

I enclose my résumé for your attention and would be pleased to attend an interview at any time convenient for you.

I look forward to hearing from you.

Yours sincerely,

Joel Redpath

1. You don't use contractions in an e-mail of application. ☐
2. You need to give details of your qualification. ☐
3. You need to state the post you are applying for. ☐
4. You should ask for an interview. ☐

2 **Read the advertisements and choose one of them to respond to. Use the e-mail you read as a reference.**

→ Qualified Hairdresser

Local saloon requires a qualified hairdresser. Hours are Tuesday and Wednesday 9:00 A.M.-5:30 P.M., Thursday 9:00 A.M.-9:00 P.M., Friday 9:00 A.M.-5:30 P.M. and Saturdays 9:00 A.M.-2:00 P.M. Duties will include cutting and colouring of hair. Experience is essential. License preferred. Salary $38,000-$40,000.

To apply, please e-mail Kerry at Working Arrangements at kerry@jobsearch.com.

»»» Delivery Driver

We are a laundry based in Bayswater looking to hire a delivery driver to work early mornings from 4 A.M. till around midday Monday, Wednesday and Friday and for about 5 hours every Saturday and Sunday, again early and finishing at 6 A.M. each day. A full license is required and your own vehicle to get to and from work. A late model van is supplied once at work. The applicants must be well presented and be able to read and write English. The job is very physical and requires some heavy lifting.

To apply, please e-mail Pauline Fritsch at The Towel Exchange on fritsch@towel.com.

Extracted from: http://jobsearch.gov.au/default.aspx

Review

1 Check the correct answer to fill in the blanks.

1. You ____________ quite sad lately. What's going on?
   a. have been ☐
   b. were ☐
   c. are being ☐
   d. didn't be ☐
2. The boys ____________ late last night. I ____________ to them.
   a. have arrived / talked ☐
   b. didn't arrive / have talked ☐
   c. arrived / didn't talk ☐
   d. were arriving / talked ☐
3. My mother ____________ already ____________ ten books.
   a. has / wrote ☐
   b. has / written ☐
   c. have / write ☐
   d. have / wrote ☐
4. Bill ____________ the sandwiches for the party yet.
   a. didn't brought ☐
   b. doesn't bring ☐
   c. hasn't brought ☐
   d. doesn't have brought ☐
5. When ____________ you ____________ Joe: yesterday or the day before?
   a. do / meet ☐
   b. did / meet ☐
   c. did / met ☐
   d. have / meet ☐
6. ____________ you ____________ Joe?
   a. Have / seen ☐
   b. Do / have seen ☐
   c. Have / see ☐
   d. Did / saw ☐
7. People ____________ on that house for months.
   a. have working ☐
   b. have been working ☐
   c. are working ☐
   d. has worked ☐
8. I ____________ in the same house since I was born.
   a. lived ☐
   b. did lived ☐
   c. have lived ☐
   d. have left ☐
9. In fact, I ____________ you for twenty years.
   a. knew ☐
   b. am knowing ☐
   c. didn't know ☐
   d. have known ☐
10. She ____________ not home from five to six o'clock yesterday.
    a. has been ☐
    b. is being ☐
    c. did be ☐
    d. was ☐

2 Read and listen to the text, and then answer the questions.

8

PATTERNS IN NATURE: AN ENIGMATIC INSPIRATION

Posted by Richie on Friday, February 25, 2011 · 21 Comments

Taking inspiration from Mother Nature isn't a bad idea. After all, nature has managed to create a complex self-sustaining system of life supporting millions of species over billions of years.

There is a lot we can learn about design from natural systems, and many designers, engineers, and thinkers over the last century have found inspiration in nature. From buildings and bridges to machines and medicine, examining the intricacies of the natural system in which we exist has aided in the development of improving almost every aspect of human life. Our relationship with nature's patterns yields both an infinitely rich display of beautiful things and a manifestation of the underlying order in our world. Enough material for many lifetimes of contemplation and study.

Extracted from: http://richworks.in/2011/02/patterns-in-nature-an-enigmatic-inspiration/#comments

WORD BANK

manage: conseguir
pattern: padrão
support: sustentar
yield: produzir

1. The text…
   a. describes how nature has created life. ☐
   b. criticizes people that reproduce natural systems in their designs. ☐
   c. states that designers have no inspiration to create their work. ☐
   d. explains how nature has been inspiring professionals with their work. ☐
   e. is an advertisement of an engineer who builds bridges. ☐
2. Check the incorrect alternatives about nature.
   a. Nature has been supporting millions of species over the years. ☐
   b. Nature has improved aspects of human life. ☐
   c. Natural systems can teach us about design. ☐
   d. Nature may be a subject of contemplation. ☐
   e. Nature can't be studied by humans. ☐

3 **Read and listen to the text, and then answer the questions.**

9

High-Speed Photography

High-speed photography isn't quite a modern application in photography. The first practical application was Eadweard Muybridge's 1878 investigation into whether horses' feet were actually all off the ground at once during a gallop [...]. The first photograph of a supersonic flying bullet was taken by the Austrian physicist Peter Salcher in Rijeka in 1886. Since then, high-speed photography has advanced a lot. Lex's works are a prime example of what one can achieve today if one has the right set of tools and the adequate knowledge and expertise on the subject, of course not to mention the control and the patience required to capture the right moment.

Extracted from: http://richworks.in/2012/06/high-speed-photography-taken-to-the-next-level-by-lex-augusteijn/

1. Which word could be translated as *na verdade* in the text context?
   a. actually ☐
   b. of course ☐
   c. since ☐
   d. today ☐
   e. right ☐

2. Check the correct alternatives according to the text.
   a. High speed is a modern application in photography. ☐
   b. High speed was first applied to photography in 1878. ☐
   c. The text explains who Lex was. ☐
   d. An Austrian physicist invented the supersonic bullet. ☐
   e. Muybridge wanted to know if a horse lifted all feet off the ground at once when galloping. ☐

WORD BANK

achieve: realizar
at once: de uma vez; ao mesmo tempo
bullet: bala
quite: completamente
tool: ferramenta
whether: se (conjunção condicional)

So far, SO GOOD?

1 **Solve the charades and write sentences about what people have already done. Follow the model.**

1.

ride a motorcycle to the beach

I've already ridden a motorcycle to the beach.

2.

____

____

3.

____

____

4.

____

____

Now that I've finished links 1 and 2, I can...

...express finished or unfinished past events.	☐ Yes!	☐ I still need to study more!
...use adverbs referring to indefinite time.	☐ Yes!	☐ I still need to study more!
...use some phrasal verbs and suffixes, recognize some "false friends," and fill out a simple application form.	☐ Yes!	☐ I still need to study more!

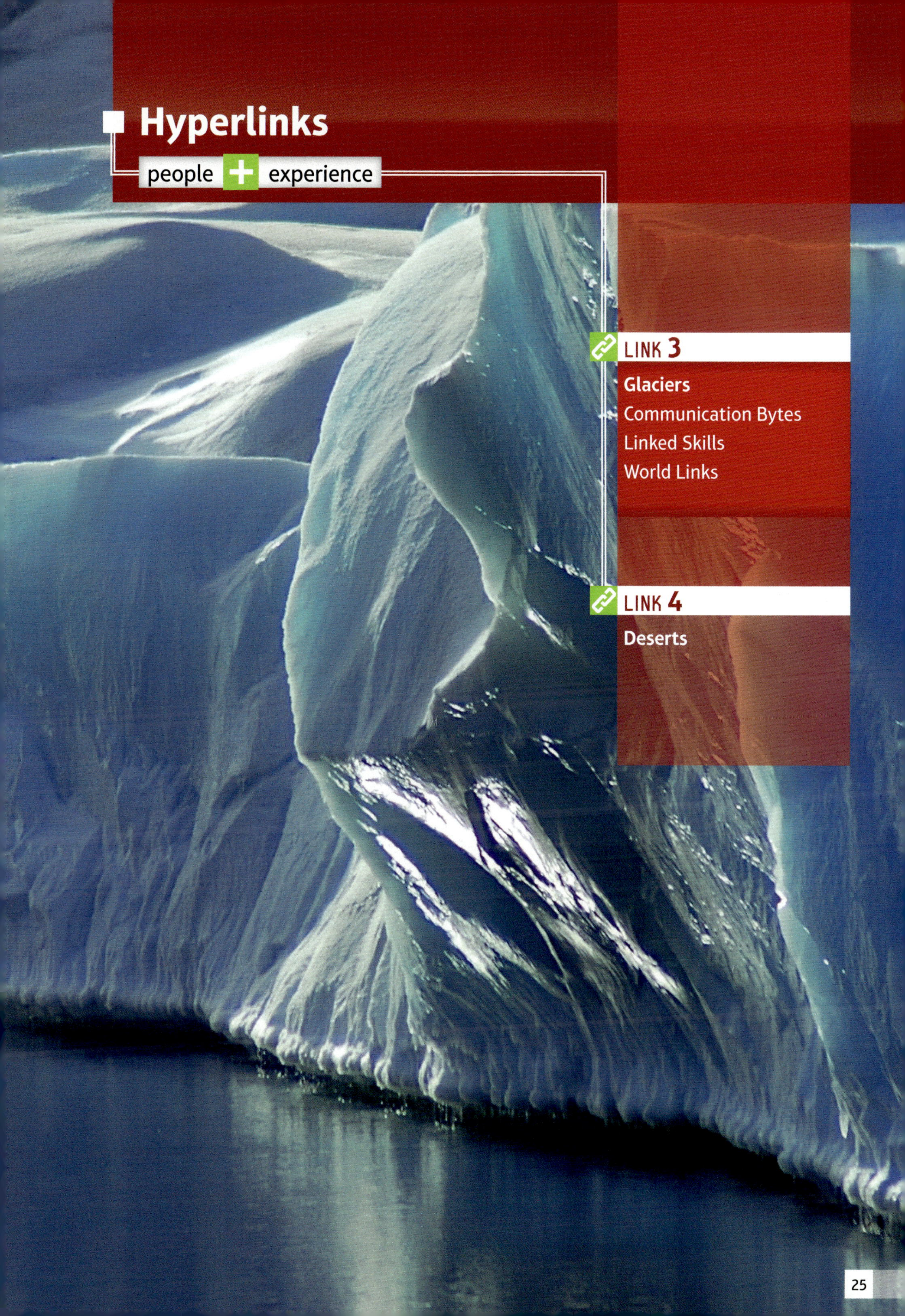

Hyperlinks

people + experience

LINK 3

Glaciers

Communication Bytes

Linked Skills

World Links

LINK 4

Deserts

LINK 3

LOG IN

1 What is Antarctica? Where is it?

2 Take a quick look at the text and answer: What are glaciers?

WORD BANK

drag: arrastar (pelo chão)
flow: fluxo
glacier: geleira
hotspot: ponto crítico
ice sheet: manto de gelo
ice shelf: plataforma de gelo (plana, espeça e flutuante)
melt: derreter
ski drag: pouso
tear: lágrima
thin (verb): afinar
warming (adjective): que está se aquecendo
warming (noun): aquecimento
worry: preocupar-se

NOTES

____

____

____

____

____

____

____

____

____

Glaciers: glaciers formed millions of years ago. They were made by falling snow which turned to ice and built up. Glaciers are just made up of ice, liquid water, and air.

10 Into Antarctica's action zone

*Glaciologist **Robert Bindschadler** and his team became the first to set foot on Antarctica's global warming hotspot – the Pine Island Glacier. He tells **Anil Ananthaswamy** what it's like to work in one of the most dangerous places on Earth.*

You have just come back from the Pine Island Glacier ice shelf in west Antarctica. What were you doing there?

This was a reconnaissance trip. I am interested in how the warming ocean is affecting the margins of the Antarctic ice sheet. [...] The Pine Island Glacier is the hotspot in the Antarctic where the ice flow into the Amundsen Sea is accelerating and the ice is thinning fastest. [...]

You have been planning this project for years. What was it like to see the ice shelf for the first time?

I had seen satellite images of the region on my computer screen countless times and from every possible angle. When I finally saw it for real, out of the window of the aircraft, it was very dramatic. [...] They did two ski drags and the third time they landed. There was a tear in my eye because I had worried so long and hard about whether it was going to be possible to land on the ice shelf. I was thrilled. [...]

What made you want to be a glaciologist in the first place?

[...] I came across a book called *The Physics of Glaciers* by Stan Paterson which I read in one night. Once I realized there was a field called glaciology, I wrote letters to people who had written papers on it and that led me to an opening in graduate school at the University of Washington, Seattle.

What do you remember about your first trip to Antarctica?

[...] My previous experience of this kind of environment had been in Alaska, where they have big mountains and glaciers, but Antarctica was on a totally different scale – 10 to 100 times bigger.

Extracted from: www.newscientist.com/article/mg19726471.900-interview-into-antarcticas-action-zone.html?full=true

UNCOVERING THE *TEXT*

TOPIC

____

GENRE

What kind of text is the one on pages 26 and 27?

- [ ] advertisement
- [ ] article
- [ ] autobiography
- [ ] interview

Summarizing is a reading strategy!

Essa estratégia consiste em expressar, de forma breve, os pontos principais de um texto.

RELATED LINKS

For more information on this Link's topics, please visit:

http://glaciology.weebly.com/
http://iaato.org/

FORUM

Do you know about any governmental measures being taken to prevent global warming?

How about you? What have you been doing about it?

1 Scan the text for information to fill in the blanks.

1. The interviewee's name: ______________________.
2. The interviewer's name: ______________________.
3. The author of *The Physics of Glaciers*: ______________________.

2 Complete the information with words from the text.

1. Glaciers are made up of ______________________.
2. Bindschadler and his team were the first to ______________________ ______________________.

3 Check the correct answer according to the text.

1. Bindschadler's trip was…
   a. an adventure trip. [ ]
   b. an inspection trip. [ ]
2. The ice is becoming thinner…
   a. on the north coast. [ ]
   b. at the Pine Island Glacier. [ ]
3. What is causing the ice to melt?
   a. The warming ocean. [ ]
   b. The cold glacier. [ ]
4. The Pine Island Glacier is…
   a. closer to the South Pole. [ ]
   b. closer to the North Pole. [ ]

4 According to what you've read, is it possible to infer that Bindschadler likes being a glaciologist?

____

5 Read the text again and complete the summary.

Robert Bindschadler, is a (1) ______________. He went to (2) ______________________, the place in Antarctica where the ice is (3) ______________________, in a (4) ______________________ trip. His (5) ______________________ experience had been in Alaska.

EXPANDING THE *VOCABULARY*

1 Write the translation of the underlined phrasal verbs. Observe the context in order to find the best translation.

1. The ice <u>built up</u> through the years, forming glaciers.
___
2. He <u>came back</u> from Antarctica after a reconnaissance trip.
___
3. Robert <u>came across</u> a book on the physics of glaciers.
___
4. Throughout the years, the falling snow <u>turned to</u> ice.
___

Phrasal Verb

É formado de um verbo mais uma partícula que modifica o significado desse verbo.

Ex.: *give* = dar;
give up = desistir.

2 Observe this sentence: "He tells Anil Ananthaswamy what it's like to work in one of the most <u>dangerous</u> places on Earth." The word *dangerous* is formed with the suffix *-ous*. Form adjectives by using the underlined words and the suffix *-ous*. Then rewrite the sentences. Study the example.

Suffixes

O sufixo *-ous* significa "característica; ter a natureza ou qualidade de" e forma adjetivos.

Ex.: *fury – furi***ous**;
*anxiety – anxi***ous**;
*fame – fam***ous**;
*virtue – virtu***ous**.

1. She has a lot of <u>ambition</u>. *ambitious*
She is very ambitious
2. He has a lot of <u>courage</u>. ___
___
3. They have a lot of <u>grace</u>. ___
___
4. Be careful, that snake has <u>poison</u>. ___
___
5. They have a lot of <u>generosity</u>. ___
___

3 Circle the suffixes of the words below to find the root words.

1. action
2. thinning
3. totally
4. glaciologist
5. fastest
6. dangerous
7. landed
8. accelerating
9. countless
10. physicist

4 **The words on the left are all from the text. Match them to the ones that are similar in meaning.**

1. just	☐ point of view
2. turn to	☐ become
3. realize	☐ form
4. build up	☐ understand
5. angle	☐ only

5 **In the sentence "You have just come back from the Pine Island Glacier ice shelf in West Antarctica," there is a phrasal verb using the verb *come*. Check the meaning of other phrasal verbs using the same verb.**

1. The kids *came down* with a virus.
   a. be afraid of ☐ b. fall ill ☐ c. fight ☐
2. She *came to* an hour after the operation.
   a. die ☐ b. leave the hospital ☐ c. become conscious ☐
3. My brother's puzzle *came apart* when I tried to lift it. I have to fix it before he arrives.
   a. arrive ☐ b. appear ☐ c. separate ☐
4. She will *come into* a lot of money when her grandmother dies.
   a. inherit ☐ b. find out ☐ c. lose ☐
5. The band's new CD is *coming out* next year.
   a. be available ☐ b. disappear ☐ c. record ☐

6 **Check possible inferences of the sentences below.**

1. When I saw the glacier for real, I couldn't believe my eyes.
   a. The person believed the glacier didn't exist. ☐
   b. The person had not seen the glacier in person before. ☐
2. I had worried so long about whether it was going to be possible to land on the ice shelf.
   a. He was sure that landing was possible. ☐
   b. He wasn't sure landing was possible. ☐
3. One day I came across a book called *The Physics of Glaciers*, which I read in one night.
   a. The book was so interesting he couldn't put it down. ☐
   b. The person had insomnia. ☐

DISCOVERING GRAMMAR

Past Perfect

I *had seen* satellite images of the region.
I wrote letters to people who *had written* papers on it.

Usamos o *Past Perfect* para indicar uma ação que ocorreu antes de outra que também está no passado, só que no *Simple Past*.

I *had cleaned* the room **when** she called me.

She *hadn't changed* clothes **before** I arrived.

He called the police **after** I *had left*.

Had he *finished* his homework **when** you arrived?

A estrutura do *Past Perfect* é similar à do *Present Perfect*. A diferença é que usamos o auxiliar *have* no passado, ou seja, *had* mais o *Past Participle* do verbo principal. Em frases negativas, acrescentamos *not* depois do auxiliar (*hadn't – contracted form*); e, em frases interrogativas, começamos com o verbo auxiliar *had*. Também temos a *contracted form* na afirmativa – por exemplo, *I had* → *I'd*.

Note

O **Past Perfect Continuous** (*had been* + verbo + *-ing*) enfatiza que a ação já durava um tempo:

I *had been working* hard when he arrived.

1 Complete the sentences with the Past Perfect of the verbs in parentheses.

1. I was exhausted because I ________________ (work) for twelve hours.
2. She ________________ already ________________ (send) him an e-mail when he phoned her.
3. We didn't realize it was your uncle, although we ________________ (see) him before.
4. They didn't get off the plane until it ________________ (stop) completely.
5. I ________________ (have) dinner when our friends arrived.
6. When the firefighters arrived, the fire ________________ (destroy) the house.
7. She felt better after she ________________ (take) the medicine.
8. The old lady's eyes were red. She ________________ (cry) before her son arrived.

2 Read the excerpt from *The Body in the Library* and underline the verbs in the Past Perfect.

Chapter 1 – A Shocking Discovery

Miss Jane Marple was a woman of between sixty and seventy who lived in a cottage close to the Vicarage. She had lived in St. Mary Mead for many years and had many friends there. She had never married, and most of the time she lived the life of an ordinary old lady.

But Miss Marple had a hobby – a very surprising one. She solved murders.

Source: The Body in the Library, by Agatha Christie, retold by Anne Collins (Penguin Active Reading, 2008, page 5)

Communication Bytes

1 **Julie, Roy, and Eddie are trying to set a time and place to meet. Listen to their conversation.**

11

Eddie: OK, folks. What time are we meeting?

Roy: At three.

Julie: You had said four.

Roy: No… yes … well… I had said four and then… three.

Eddie: Sorry. I didn't follow that. What time did you say?

Roy: Three. I changed from four to three, at the school library.

Julie: You had said at the lab.

Eddie: Sorry, again. Where exactly are we to meet?

Julie: I prefer the lab!

Eddie: Three is too early for me. How about five?

Roy: OK, OK, let's start over again.

2 **Write T for *true* or F for *false*.**

1. They will meet at the lab. ☐
2. They are not sure about the time and place for meeting. ☐
3. They agree about the time and place. ☐
4. They don't agree about place but agree about time. ☐

3 **When we don't understand what people say, we can ask for clarification. Talk to a friend about a time and place to meet and ask for clarification. The words and expressions below may help.**

Sorry, could you repeat that, please?	Where exactly…?
Excuse me. What was that again?	What do you mean by…?
Could you say that again, please?	What do you mean?
I didn't follow that. Could you repeat it?	(Informal) What? I didn't catch that.
What time did you say?	

Linked Skills

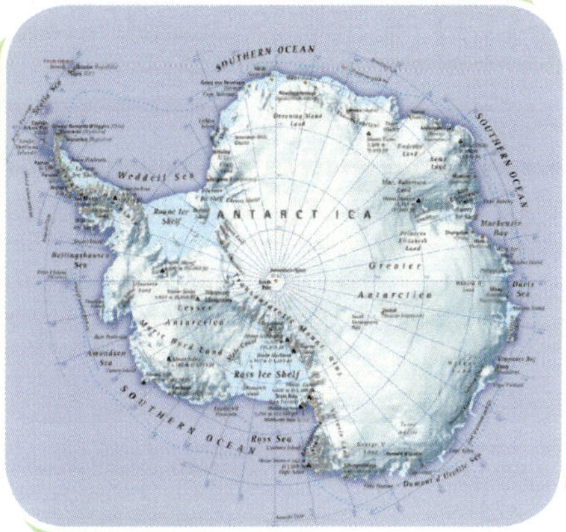

1 **Listen to part of a radio program about Antarctica and match the information.** (12)

1. Marinus of Tyre
2. ancient Greeks
3. 1840s
4. Robert Falcon Scott
5. reserved for science and protected from territorial claims

- [ ] first time when humans actually saw Antarctica
- [ ] person who gave Antarctica its name
- [ ] person who died when returning from the South Pole
- [ ] Antarctica
- [ ] believed in the existence of a southern land

2 **Amyr Klink is a Brazilian sailor who has already traveled to many parts of the world, including Antarctica. Use the information to write a paragraph about him. You can use the transcript of the first exercise for help.**

name: Amyr Khan Klink
born: September 25th, 1955; Paraty, Rio de Janeiro State
Invernagem Antárctica em Solitário
Start of the project: December 1989.
27,000 miles sailing from Antarctica to the Arctic
642 days traveling
two books about it: *Paratii – entre dois polos* and *As janelas do Paratii*

3 **Compare your paragraph to your partner's.**

13

Cruising Antarctica

So you want to see Antarctica before it melts into the Southern Ocean? Put your hitching thumb back in your pocket and reach for your wallet instead. Getting there isn't cheap or easy, but it's totally worth it for increasing numbers of curious adventurers.

What's On the Agenda? Though expeditions vary, here's what you can expect on most cruises to Antarctica:

1. Trips primarily go to ice-free coastal zones from November to March, during the continent's summer. Days are long (up to 20-plus hours), and temps can occasionally climb into the 40s (F) along the peninsula. The temperatures in the Ross Sea region are cooler.

2. Basically, you sail across a lot of water to your first destination. During the passage, educate and entertain yourself by attending onboard presentations on topics such as seabirds, whales, seals, geology, glaciology, history, and even photography. Any worthy trip includes experts in Antarctica, such as naturalists and scientists.

3. Weather and ice rule! Plans and itineraries can change on the fly. A good captain work with Mother Nature, not against her.

4. The crew transports passengers from the ship to land in Zodiac landing craft (rubbe rafts with motors). Zodiac cruises also provide great views of icebergs and wildlife.

5. Landings are typically geared toward penguin colonies, historic sites, research stations, and interesting terrain and features.

6. For a fee, some ships offer extra adventures. Ask about kayaking & camping. Let's not talk about climbing & diving!

7. Unless you have salt in your veins, you'll probably feel a little sea-sick at some point on the journey. The Drake Passage can be a wild ride or, if you're lucky, Drake Lake. Be prepared just in case. Not sure how to change this, but I don't think we should tell people they will get sick, just to prepare for the possibility of seasickness...

8. Is there a doctor on board? Yes, of course. But don't plan on any serious injuries because it's a long evacuation back to civilization!

9. Forget the discos, casinos, and glitzy dance shows of mainstream cruise lines. This is about the wildlife, scenery, education and new friends.

Think about it!

There have been some measures concerning the fuel used in ships that cruise Antarctica. They have gone more sustainable, but more expensive, which decreased the amount of people visiting the continent. What's your opinion about this? Should they keep the decision in order to avoid great disasters like oil leaks or try to encourage tourism and use regular fuel?

Extracted from http://www.polarcruises.com/polar-info/antarctica-info/cruising-antarctica

10. You don't need documentation or visas to visit Antarctica, unless you land at other countries en route that require them.

11. Whether on shore, in a zodiac, or on board the ship, passengers can expect close encounters with penguins, seals, and sea birds and if you get lucky, maybe even a whale or two! Bring your camera and be ready for an eyeful!

Attention!

There are many cruise options to Antarctica. If you are interested, you can search for more information on tourism agencies where you live.

World links

Reading Comprehension

1 **Write T for *true*, F for *false*, and NS if the information is *not stated* in the text.**

1. One can easily get to Antarctica. ☐
2. You need documentation to land at other countries en route. ☐
3. The schedule might change due to weather conditions. ☐
4. From November to March, it's the continent's winter. ☐
5. It's impossible to visit Antarctica during winter. ☐

2 **Scan the text to answer the questions below.**

1. How can one get to land when on a cruise in Antarctica?

___

2. Unless you are very used to traveling in ships, you'll probably suffer from what kind of illness?

___

3. Are there many variations on cruises to Antarctica? Justify, using part of the text.

___

___

4. What kind of attractions can you find on a cruise to Antarctica?

___

5. What kinds of animals are easily found when on a cruise to Antarctica?

___

3 **In a ship or airplane, the crew is made up of people working, providing services for the customers. Can you identify two different kinds of crew members you will find on a cruise to Antarctica?**

___

4 **What can you infer from the following sentence: "Put your hitching thumb back in your pocket and reach for your wallet instead"?**

1. You will spend a lot of money in order to go on a cruise to Antarctica. ☐
2. You need documents to go to Antarctica. ☐
3. It's very unlikely that you will reach Antarctica if you are hitchhiking. ☐

5 **Continue reading the text and write a sentence that confirms your inference.**

___

Hyperlinks

people + experience

LINK 4

LOG IN

1 What are deserts?

2 Where are there deserts?

WORD BANK

bear: suportar
cast off: livrar-se de
fierce: feroz
freedom: liberdade
gathering: reunião
hiking: caminhada do tipo *trekking*
hunting: caça
stunning: deslumbrante
whisper: sussurro
wonder: maravilha
yoke: jugo, peso

NOTES

____

____

____

____

____

____

____

____

____

____

(14)

The Sahara Desert

Deserts

Most agree that "desert areas" are those with less than 250 mm (10 in.) of rainfall on average during the year. [...] In contrast to popular belief, sand is not commonplace in deserts. Most often, small rocks, pebbles, or loose gravel form the surface layer [...]: only 15 per cent of the world's desert surface consists of pure sand [...] .

The Sahara Desert is the world's largest hot desert, covering much of North Africa. [...]

People and Cultures

According to estimates, the Sahara's entire population probably equals less than two million people, including those who live in permanent communities near water sources, those who move from place to place with the seasons, and those who follow the ancient trade routes as permanent nomads. Most have Berber and/or Arabic roots. The Berbers, speaking several dialects of the Berber language, appeared on the scene at the dawn of the Sahara's history. [...] Most of the Sahara's population follows the Islamic religion, introduced in the seventh century A.D.

The Sahara's history is written in terms of primitive hunting and gathering, nomadic trade, agricultural development, early communities, conquest, sophisticated civilizations, monumental architecture, dynasty, exploration, colonization, and war. It bears the stamp not only of the Berbers and early Arabs, but also of Egyptians, Nubians, Phoenicians, Greeks, and Romans. In more recent centuries, it experienced the imprint of Ottoman, Spanish, Italian, French, and English colonialism. In the nineteenth century, it heard the whisper of Roman Catholicism. During World War II, it suffered fierce and destructive battles between the Germans and the Allies. In the middle of the last century, its countries cast off their colonial yokes and found freedom.

Wonders

The Sahara, with its natural and cultural wonders, offers the tourist a rich travel experience. [...] you can:

- Explore dune fields, oases, the Nile and Niger rivers [...].
- Join hiking and camel treks [...].
- Visit stunning monuments [...], for instance, the standing ruins of ancient cultures and the edifices of more recent cultures.
- Enjoy the rich fare of ancient, but still lively, bazaars and marketplaces.

If you have not traveled in the Sahara and you are not familiar with the local conventions and standards, you should consult a travel agent, who should provide the information you will need for a rewarding trip.

By Jay W. Sharp

Extracted from: Jim Flegg, Deserts – A Miracle of Life (New York, Facts on File, 1993; pp. 32, 33) www.desertusa.com/du_sahara_life.html

UNCOVERING THE *TEXT*

TOPIC

___

GENRE

What kind of text is on pages 38 and 39?

- [ ] advertisement
- [ ] article
- [ ] legend
- [ ] technical essay

Recognizing text genre is a Reading strategy!

Identificar o gênero textual nos ajuda a prever estruturas, o que, por sua vez, facilita nossa navegação pelo texto.

1 **Where can you possibly find this kind of text? Justify your answer.**

___

2 **According to the map, into how many countries does the Sahara Desert extend? Name them.**

___

___

3 **Read the sentences and find evidence in the text to support or contradict them. Then mark T for *true* or F for *false* and write the sentence that made you decide.**

1. The Sahara is a large desert in North Africa. [ ]

___

2. The Sahara's population has just Arabic roots. [ ]

___

3. Catholicism strongly influenced the Sahara's population in the nineteenth century. [ ]

___

4. There are cultural marvels to be explored in the Sahara. [ ]

___

RELATED LINKS

For more information on this Link's topics, please visit:

http://www.bbc.co.uk/nature/habitats/Deserts_and_xeric_shrublands
http://www.telegraph.co.uk/news/newstopics/howaboutthat/4357553/Top-5-best-complaint-letters.html

FORUM

In extreme environments such as deserts, human life is only possible in strong communities. Do you think life in the city could be better if we saw each other as part of the same community?

EXPANDING THE *VOCABULARY*

1 **Write the words under the correct pictures.**

sand   desert rocks   pebbles   loose gravel

______________   ______________   ______________   ______________

2 **Read the text again. Check the best translation or meaning for the underlined words.**

1. The Berbers appeared on the scene at the dawn of the Sahara's history.
   - a. começo do dia ☐
   - b. fim do dia ☐
   - c. final de tarde ☐
   - d. começo; aurora ☐
2. The Sahara's history is written in terms of primitive hunting and gathering, nomadic trade, agricultural development, early communities [...].
   - a. primitivo ☐
   - b. cedo ☐
   - c. adiantado ☐
   - d. logo ☐
3. In contrast to popular belief, sand is not commonplace in deserts.
   - a. rare ☐
   - b. something ordinary ☐
   - c. something uncommon ☐
   - d. unusual ☐

3 **Circle the suffixes of the words below, and then check the correct alternatives.**

Egyptians   Ottomans   Germans   Nubians   Phoenicians   English

Spanish   Italians   Islamism   Catholicism   colonialism   Romans

1. The suffixes *-ian*, *-an*, and *-ish* mean...
   - a. what country a person, thing, or language comes from. ☐
   - b. showing the ability to. ☐
   - c. a set of beliefs. ☐
2. The suffix *-ism* means...
   - a. a process or its result. ☐
   - b. a set of beliefs. ☐
   - c. status, power. ☐
   - d. the state or quality of. ☐

4 **Classify the underlined words as A (adjective), N (noun), or V (verb).**

1. The Sahara's history is written in terms of primitive hunting ☐ and gathering ☐.
2. It experienced the imprint of Ottoman, French ☐, and English colonialism.
3. It suffered destructive battles between the Germans ☐ and the Allies.
4. Small ☐ rocks, pebbles, or loose gravel form ☐ the surface layer.

5 **All the words in the box were taken from the text. Match them to their opposites.**

stunning	freedom	permanent	fierce	monumental	loose

1. ugly: ____________________
2. insignificant: ____________________
3. peaceful: ____________________
4. tight: ____________________
5. captivity: ____________________
6. temporary: ____________________

6 **Refer to the pictures below using words from exercise 5.**

1. 

Monument Valley, in Utah and Arizona, offers its visitors a ____________________ view.

2. 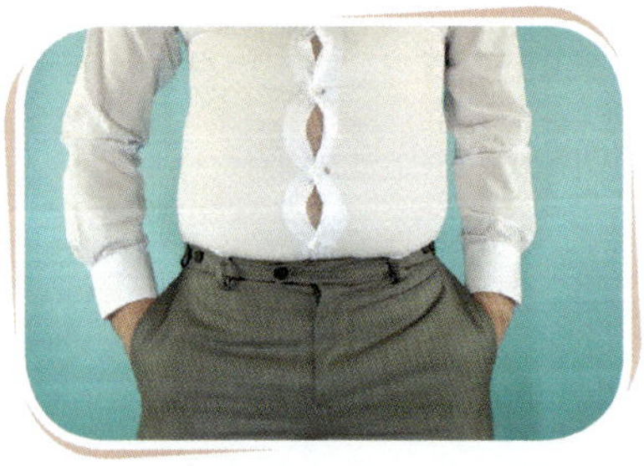

That is a little bit ____________________, isn't it?

3. 

That is a(an) ____________________ storm.

DISCOVERING *GRAMMAR*

Gerund, Infinitive, & Participle

The Sahara's history is written in terms of primitive *hunting*.
The Berbers, *speaking* several dialects of the Berber language [...].
You should *consult* a travel agent.

A partícula *to* colocada antes de um verbo indica seu *Infinitive*; entretanto, o *Infinitive* pode aparecer com ou sem *to*. Após verbos modais, *would rather*, *had better*, *but*, e *except*, usamos o *Infinitive* sem *to*.

You must *go*. / I'd better *stay*.

Após verbo *to be* + adjetivo e após alguns verbos e expressões (por exemplo, *the first*, *ask*, *decide*, *intend* etc.), usamos o *Infinitive* com *to*.

I'm happy *to be* here. / She was the first *to arrive*.

Forma negativa: acrescentamos *not* antes do verbo no *Infinitive* ou antes da partícula *to* quando ela está presente.

I decided *not* to go.

A terminação *-ing* acrescentada a um verbo pode formar seu *Gerund* ou seu *Present Participle*. O *Gerund* é usado para formar substantivos; após preposições; e após alguns verbos e expressões (por exemplo, *go*, *stop*, *can't stand* etc.).

Hunting is not my pastime. / He left without *crying*.

Forma negativa: acrescentamos *no/not* antes do verbo no *Gerund*.

No smoking here!

O *Present Participle* é usado para formar tempos contínuos e para formar adjetivos.

She is a *working* woman.

1 Match the columns.

1. He traveled to Australia
2. She's studying hard
3. He spoke softly

( ) not to wake the baby.
( ) to pass her exams.
( ) to visit his relatives.

2 Complete the sentences with the verbs from the box.

date be laugh dance

1. Hannah practiced ________________ the samba for two months before Carnival.
2. Vanessa dislikes ________________ in front of the computer all day long.
3. She should ________________ that boy. He's so nice.
4. You must ________________ sure about it before saying such things.

Letter of complaint

1 **Read the letter of complaint and answer.**

15

Mr. Sunders,

I have just arrived at the hotel I booked at your travel agency, but unfortunately I already feel the need to write this letter of complaint. The hotel is nothing like you showed me before I traveled. The pictures were outdated, as the hotel is in poor repair. And worst of all: the air conditioning system is not working. As I'm visiting the Sahara Desert, you can imagine this is a very hot place, and my family and I are suffering without an air conditioner.

I would have written an e-mail, but guess what? No Internet connection around here. I hope you take the appropriate measures as soon as you receive this letter and put us in a better hotel.

Sincerely,

Mr. Adams

1. Check the problems Mr. Adams states in his letter.
   a. The air conditioner doesn't work. ☐
   b. There's no Internet connection. ☐
   c. Room service was not efficient. ☐
   d. The hotel is more expensive than he expected it to be. ☐
2. What does it mean to say the hotel "is in poor repair"?
   a. The hotel is in good condition. ☐
   b. The hotel needs small adjustments. ☐
   c. The building is not in good condition. ☐

2 **Write a letter complaining about a problem with your luggage, as you are already at your hotel but it hasn't arrived yet. You can use the previous letter and the topics to help you.**

Identify yourself and the service you were expecting.

State the problem: be clear about what's wrong.

Propose a solution: tell the company what you want them to do to solve your problem.

Review

1 Choose the best alternative to complete the sentences.

1. Most people in North Africa are ______. The religion they believe in is called Islam. ______ pray five times a day ______ the city of Mecca.
   a. Muslims; Muslims; facing ☐
   b. Muslim; Muslims; to face ☐
   c. Muslims; Muslims; to facing ☐
2. In countries south of the Sahara Desert, the majority of the people are ______. Some people, however, choose ______ ancient religions and ______ that natural spirits and ancestors affect everyday life.
   a. Christian; follow; believe ☐
   b. Christians; following; to believe ☐
   c. Christian; to follow; believe ☐
3. Christianity ________ present in Africa for several centuries before Arab Muslims ______ around 680 A.D.
   a. had been; have arrived ☐
   b. had been; arrived ☐
   c. have been; have arrived ☐
4. More than a thousand different languages are spoken in Africa. Due to their colonial pasts, most countries in West Africa ________ French, English, Spanish, or Portuguese as ______ languages.
   a. have adopted; nationality ☐
   b. had adopted; national ☐
   c. have adopted; national ☐
5. Most inhabitants also speak indigenous languages. Cameroonians may ______ one or more of twenty-four different languages, in addition to French or English.
   a. speak ☐ b. to speak ☐ c. speaking ☐
6. Dunes ______ also ______ the subject of many desert movies. Dune deserts ______ one of the most beautiful or the most inhospitable places on Earth.
   a. has; been; can be ☐ b. has; been; can to be ☐ c. have; been; can be ☐
7. For centuries, explorers throughout the world ________ strange sounds ________ from sand dunes.
   a. have described; to emanate ☐
   b. have describing; emanating ☐
   c. have described; emanating ☐
8. The sounds ________ variously described as ____________.
   a. have been; singing and booming ☐
   b. have been; sing and boom ☐
   c. has been; singing and booming ☐
9. One of the best places ______ ______ dunes in the western United States is Sand Mountain.
   a. observing; booming ☐ b. observe; to boom ☐ c. to observe; booming ☐

Sources: www.desertusa.com/magjan98/dunes/jan_dune1.html; www.africanculturalcenter.org/5_3languages_religion.html

2 The following texts are (1) an answer to an American student who asked why Antarctica is not considered the biggest desert on Earth and (2) part of an article about Antarctica's Dry Valleys. Read them and answer the questions.

16

1

Dear John,

You are quite correct to point out that Antarctica is a desert. It is what is known as a cold desert, which is probably why you find that it is not classified along with hot deserts like the Sahara. [...]

The entire continent is [...] a vast cold desert. It is, as you rightly say, larger than the Sahara (Antarctica is about 14.2 million square kilometres in size, and the Sahara is just over 9 million square kilometres).

As you rightly point out, Antarctica is clearly the largest desert on Earth. The reason you do not often see it listed along with hot deserts is mainly, I suspect, just that people think of deserts as hot.

Best wishes,

David Scarboro

Extracted from: www.madsci.org/posts/archives/2001-10/1003424658.Es.r.html

2

17

Dry Valleys

The Dry Valleys are an Antarctic anomaly. While most of the continent is covered in a thick layer of ice, the dry, frigid Valleys are almost entirely ice-free, an arid expanse of mostly dirt, small rocks, and big boulders. [...]

Research has shown that the Dry Valleys offer scientists more than a laboratory for studying Earth. The Valleys are Earth's closest equivalent to Mars. Both planets have polar caps, valleys, rivers, and lakes, and the coldest temperatures in the Valleys come close to temperatures on Mars. The two places have a lot in common.

What can the Valleys teach us about Mars? There are lots of questions scientists are pursuing, but perhaps the most intriguing is whether or not we'll find life there. [...]

Extracted from: http://icestories.exploratorium.edu/dispatches/big-ideas/dry-valleys/

1. What question would fit best according to the reply letter that David Scarboro wrote John?
   a. My teacher said Antarctica is a desert, but I don't believe it. Is it true? ☐
   b. Antarctica is a desert and it's bigger than the Sahara, so why is it not usually listed among the largest deserts on Earth? ☐
2. Choose two sentences from the letter to justify your previous answer.

____

____

____

3. Based on the second text, write T for *true* or F for *false* for each sentence.
   a. NASA has many reasons to study the Dry Valleys. ☐
   b. The things that can be learned in the Dry Valleys are meaningful only to our own planet. ☐
   c. The Dry Valleys are an abnormality in Antarctica because they are an ice-free, hot place. ☐

4. Read the two texts again and summarize both of them in a paragraph. A good summary must be clear and straight to the point. You must write one paragraph linking both ideas, not treating them as separate texts. Use the information from the box to help you write it.

- A summary begins with an introductory sentence that states the article's title and author.
- A summary is written in your own words. It contains few or no quotes.
- A summary is always shorter than the original text, often about one-third as long as the original.
- A summary should contain all the major points of the original text and ignore most of the fine details, examples, illustrations, or explanations.
- A summary must contain only the ideas of the original text. Do not insert any of your own opinions, interpretations, deductions, or comments into a summary.

____

____

____

____

____

____

So far, SO GOOD?

1 Create nouns or adjectives using the words below and find them in the crossword puzzle. Follow the model.

1. meet ____________________
2. begin ____________________
3. fascinate ____________________
4. warm ____________________
5. dance ____________________
6. talk ___*talking*___

Z B Y Y S L P Q W H J R A E Y J I M S C
M S U L I F G M M U W F T P L Z X U H I
T A S Q E A Y M A T N N I Y S M W Y N K
E A R S P S E I X T W C K B U L P D O V
V S D C I C A E G I L G H R G L L S T Y
E I A R F I A M C N T S X G N Y V A T S
H N N Q L N L H I A L A J N I Y C P A W
I H C D E A U Z L X N W B U T Y E J L U
X A I K D T A H D S O D H Y E M Y S K Y
E J N P S I O L G Y L R G P E P V K I X
D D G I Z N V E F X X N P L M I G C N H
I B O A B G L X C N I I X P L P X A G U
V X J T O X H R V N X Z W Y A Y W F B H
L P M N J B V T N B Z G Z E M J W Z U I
B D Z Y M W E I G C L D J I K Q C W A K
G D O S O Z G N X D W A R M I N G N E Q
Y K U R M E C B T A G W V T A B J G M W
B K R V B R M T T I Y L D A S P Y X C N
C Z A H W A B T E E R K N N K C K Z V Z
K N I S P N V S C N J X L O H T S K D O
N A M M X B H Q A G M E I Y T U Z A S F
Y I Y O J F N P C P K W X Q G W N B M Y

2 Using the words you created, complete the following sentences.

1. The ____________________ ocean is affecting the margins of the Antarctic ice sheet.
2. Sand dunes are one of the most ____________________ natural phenomena.
3. Don't forget we have a ____________________ to discuss our school project.
4. ____________________ is a lot of fun and also a great way to exercise because you move all your body when practicing it.

Now that I've finished links 3 and 4, I can...

...use infinitives, gerunds, and participles.	☐ Yes!	☐ I still need to study more!
...express myself about past actions in more complex sentences.	☐ Yes!	☐ I still need to study more!
...recognize and use suffixes in general.	☐ Yes!	☐ I still need to study more!

Hyperlinks

air + energy

LINK 5

LINK 6

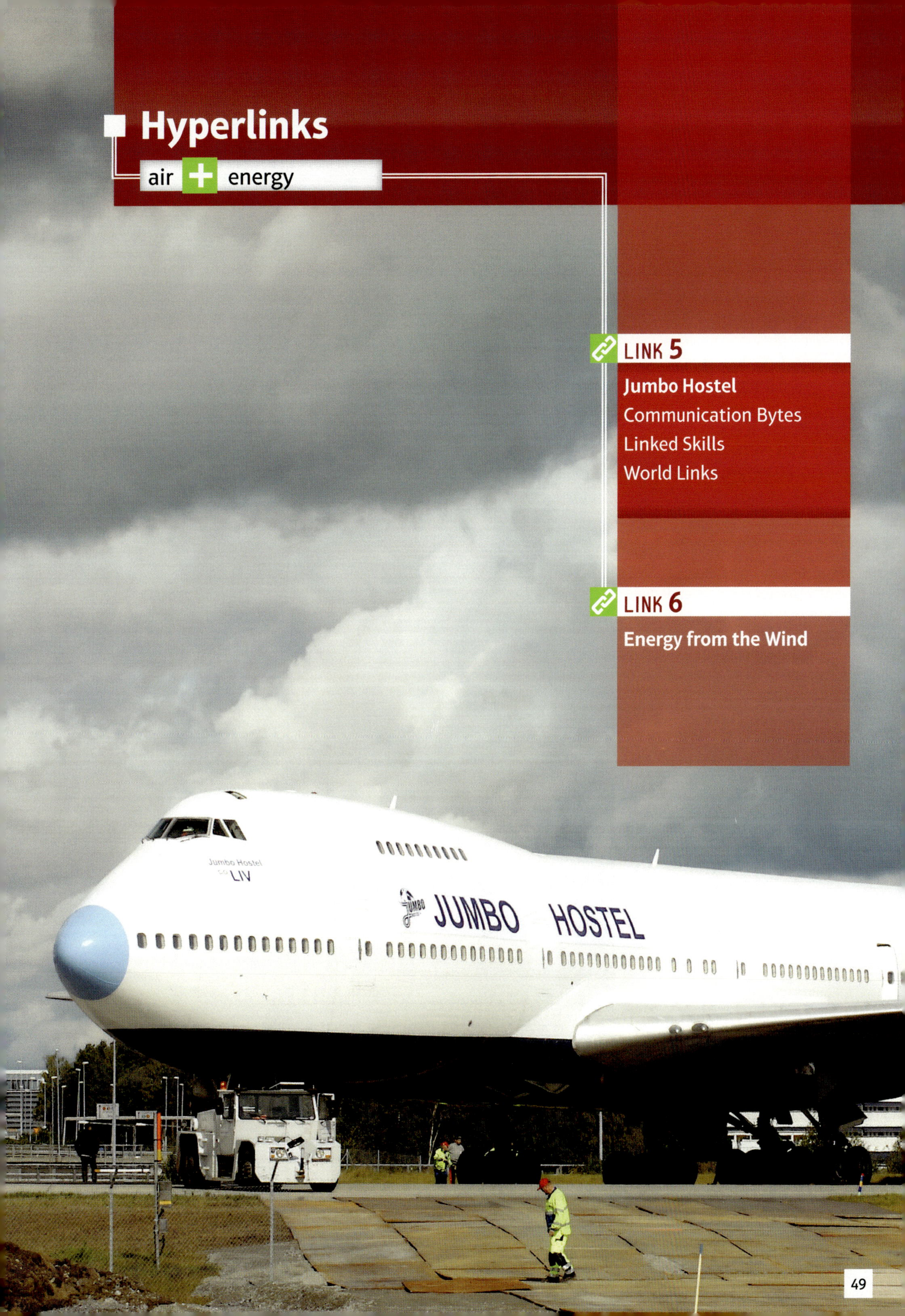

LINK 5

LOG IN

1 What do you think happens to old airplanes?

2 If you were to build a hotel, where would it be?

WORD BANK

cool: legal
entrepreneur: empreendedor
gutted: vazio, oco
jumbo (adjective): muito grande (coloquial)
runway: pista de pouso e decolagem
scrap: sucata

NOTES

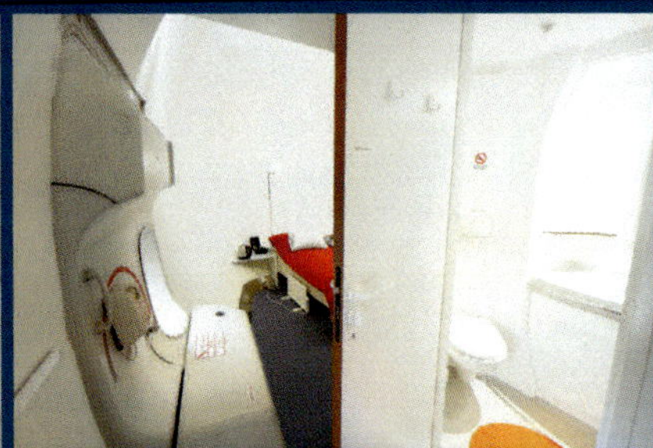

Welcome to the Hotel 747

BY DAVE DEMERJIAN

09.03.08 5:11 PM

When a jumbo jet dies (and plenty of them do these days), it's usually sold for scrap or sent to bake in the desert until the end of time. But Swedish entrepreneur Oscar Dios has a better idea for the 30-year-old junker he bought – turn it into a hostel.

Dios is stuffing 85 beds into a gutted Boeing 747 he's dubbed Jumbo Hostel and parked right outside Stockholm's Arlanda Airport. It's got 25 rooms, with some of the nicest on the plane's upper floor. But if you're looking for a romantic evening with someone special [...] you'll want the deluxe cockpit suite. It's bigger, it's got its own bathroom, and it offers a stunning view of the runway.

While most of the rooms have shared bathrooms and showers, they've all got heat and air conditioning, WiFi and – in a nod to the airplane geeks surely making reservations – flatscreen televisions that double as departure/arrival monitors.

On the downside, the rooms at the Jumbo Hostel are anything but – most are 20 feet square [1.86 square meter] with nine-foot [2.7-meter] ceilings. Considering there are three beds to a room, that's quite a squeeze, particularly if you're bunking with strangers. But, really, if you're looking for a place where you can stretch out and kick back, an airplane shouldn't be your first choice.

Turning an old plane into a place to spend the night is cool. But turning it into a place where we can afford to spend the night is even cooler.

[...]

Nothing in Sweden is cheap, and the Jumbo Hostel – which is slated to open by the end of the year – isn't talking room rates at this point. But we have a feeling that this is the kind of place even a wandering backpacker might be able to afford.

Extracted from: www.wired.com/autopia/2008/09/welcome-to-the-2/

UNCOVERING THE *TEXT*

TOPIC

____

GENRE

What kind of text is on page 51?

- [ ] article
- [ ] biography
- [ ] form
- [ ] instruction manual

Skimming is a reading strategy!

Ao passarmos os olhos sobre um texto, podemos ter uma ideia do assunto tratado mesmo antes de lê-lo.

RELATED LINKS

For more information on this Link's topics, please visit:

http://www.weirdandwonderful-hotels.com/

http://heralddaily.com/2009/11/11/13-repurposed-dwellings/

FORUM

What are the benefits an action like this can bring? Can you think of other objects that might be reused in a creative way, in order to avoid waste and even make profit out of it?

1 Skim the text and answer the questions.

1. Who wrote the article? ______________________
2. What time was it published? ______________________

2 Read the text and say what the underlined pronouns refer to.

1. ...it's usually sold for scrap...: ______________________
2. ...junker he bought...: ______________________
3. It's bigger...: ______________________
4. ...they've all got heat...: ______________________
5. ... that's quite a squeeze...: ______________________
____
6. But turning it into a place...: ______________________
7. ... feeling that this is the kind of place...: ______________________

3 Choose the correct answer.

1. The text is about...
   a. an old hotel. [ ] b. an old airplane. [ ]
2. The rooms are...
   a. small. [ ] b. quite comfortable. [ ]
3. According to the article, Dios's idea is...
   a. interesting. [ ] b. daring. [ ]
4. The author of the article believes the prices will be...
   a. affordable. [ ] b. quite high. [ ]

4 Scan the text and say what the following refer to.

1. thirty: ______________________
2. eighty-five: ______________________
3. Arlanda: ______________________
4. twenty-five: ______________________
5. twenty square feet: ______________________
6. Stockholm: ______________________
7. Sweden: ______________________

EXPANDING THE *VOCABULARY*

1 Find the following phrasal verbs in the text and choose the correct meaning for each of them.

1. turn…into (line 3)
   a. transform ☐ b. become ☐ c. deliver ☐
2. look for (line 6)
   a. encounter ☐ b. search ☐ c. find ☐
3. trick out (line 19)
   a. invent ☐ b. provide ☐ c. trade ☐

2 Label the pictures using words from the box. Use a dictionary to help you.

aisle overhead compartment seat seat belt
flight attendant cockpit carry-on folding table

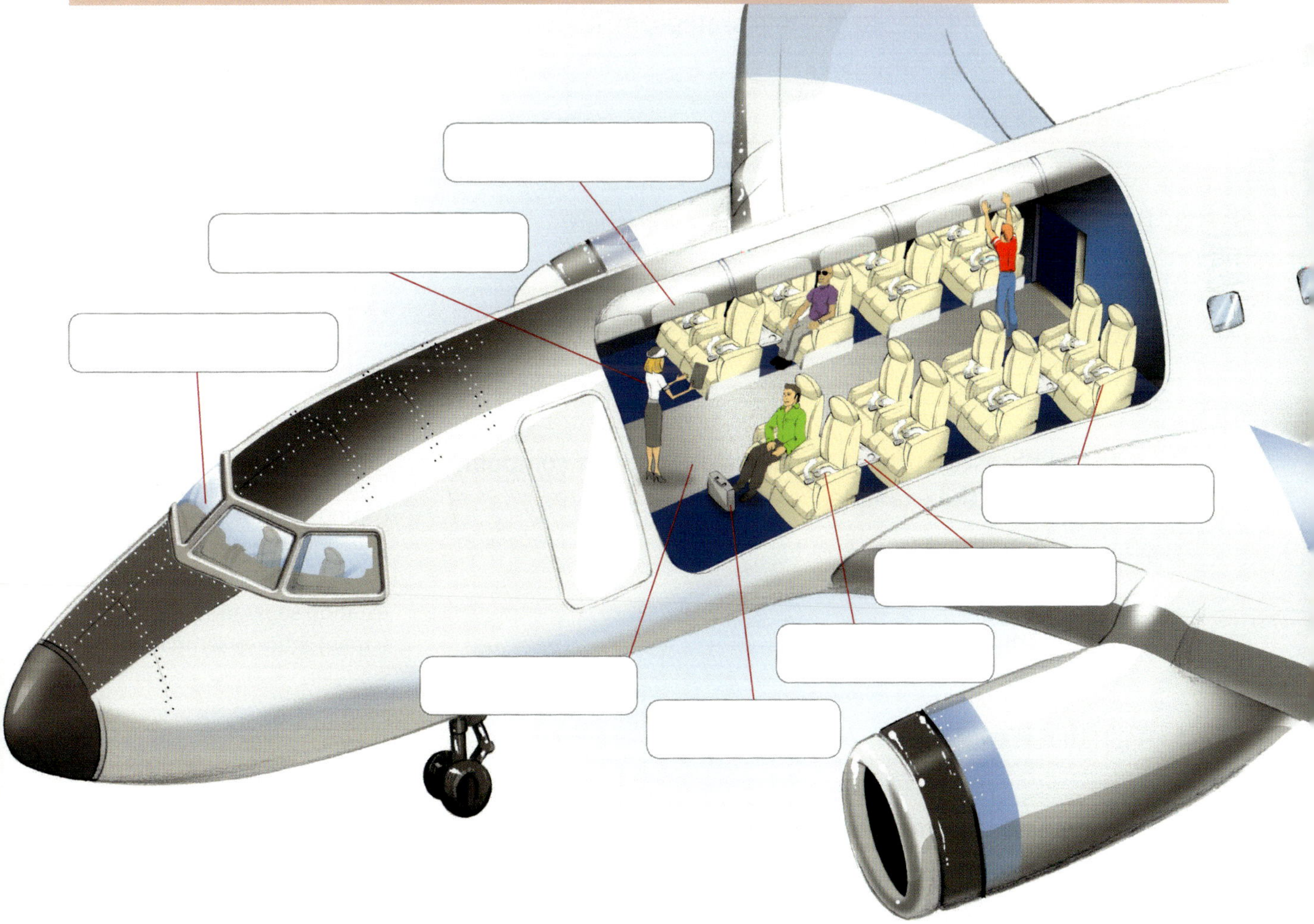

3 **Look at the following sentence: "It would have been easy for Dios to trick out his plane with ten luxury suites, tow it into downtown Stockholm, and sell it as an overpriced boutique hotel for the beautiful people." Use the prefix *over-* as in *overpriced* to form new words from the ones in the box and use them in the sentences.**

Prefixes

O prefixo *over-* transmite a ideia de excesso. Ex.: ***over**priced*, ***over**work*, ***over**do*.

price sleep cook qualify

1. The hotel was expensive, but it wasn't so nice. I think it was ______________________.
2. Jonathan has too many certificates and diplomas. I'm afraid he's ______________________ for the post.
3. How long was the meat in the oven? I'm sure it's ______________________.
4. You have to be in the office early tomorrow. Set the alarm clock so that you don't ______________.

4 **Choose the best word to complete the sentences.**

1. I can't ______________ to buy that skateboard. It's too expensive.
   a. afford ☐ b. affordable ☐
2. I don't think this restaurant is ______________ to many people.
   a. access ☐ b. accessible ☐
3. Do you think we can ______________ on Jonathan?
   a. rely ☐ b. reliable ☐
4. There was no surprise at the end of the movie. It was totally ______________.
   a. predict ☐ b. predictable ☐

5 **Rewrite the phrases, turning the description into a compound adjective. Follow the example.**

Para formarmos o adjetivo composto, usamos os elementos da descrição, que se transformam em adjetivos, estando separados por hífen e mantendo-se sempre no singular.

1. A Jumbo that is thirty years old is…
   a thirty-year-old Jumbo.
2. A building that is nine feet tall is…
   ______________________.
3. A girl that is twelve years old is…
   ______________________.
4. A room that is five meters wide is…
   ______________________.
5. A hostel that is twenty square feet is…
   ______________________.

DISCOVERING *GRAMMAR*

Comparative and Superlative

But turning it into a place where we can afford to spend the night is even *cooler*.
It's got 25 rooms, with some of the *nicest* on the plane's upper floor.

Usamos o *comparative* ao compararmos duas pessoas, animais, objetos ou situações, ou dois grupos compostos desses elementos. Ao falarmos que um é mais que outro, usamos duas estruturas diferentes, dependendo da quantidade de sílabas do adjetivo a comparar:

Para palavras com mais de duas sílabas – *beautiful*, *intelligent*, *interesting* etc. –, usamos *more* ___ *than* (mais que). She isn't *more beautiful than* her sister.

Para palavras com uma ou duas sílabas – *big*, *hot*, *simple*, *safe* etc. –, adicionamos *-er* ao final da palavra e mantemos o uso de *than*. Are zebras *stronger than* lions?

Ao compararmos um elemento com o grupo do qual faz parte, usamos o *superlative*. Também temos duas estruturas que dependem do número de sílabas da característica a comparar:

Para palavras com mais de duas sílabas, usamos *the most* ___.

This is the *most interesting exposition* ever.

Para palavras com uma ou duas sílabas, usamos *the* e adicionamos *-est* ao final da palavra.

Today is *the hottest* day this week.

Spelling:

Em palavras terminadas em consoante + vogal + consoante, dobra-se a consoante:

big – bigger – biggest

Em palavras terminadas em consoante + *y*, troca-se o *y* por *i*:

funny – funnier – funniest

Algumas palavras são exceção às regras apresentadas. Por isso, são chamadas irregulares:

good – better – best / bad – worse – worst

1 Fill in the blanks with the comparative or superlative form of the words in parentheses.

1. São Paulo is ________________________ (crowded) Campinas.
2. Sofas are ________________________ (comfortable) chairs.
3. Dancing is ________________________ (enjoyable) pastime I know.

2 Read the following words and compare them. Use your own ideas.

1. Cities / countryside

____

2. Soccer / basketball

____

Communication Bytes

1 **Camila meets her friend Julia after quite some time, and they talk about what Julia has done recently. Listen and read their conversation.** (19)

J: Hi, Camila! It's been a long time.

C: Hi, Julia! That's true! Where have you been?

J: I've been traveling.

C: That's so nice! How was it?

J: I loved it! I really enjoy meeting new people, visiting new places, and getting to know different ways of living.

C: That really sounds great!

J: Well, that's true! But it's also good to be back—after all, there are some downsides of traveling as well. For example, not sleeping in my bed, sharing the bedroom or bathroom with other people, not eating my mother's food…

C: Your mother sure is a great cook! I don't like my mother's cooking very much. But I love when my father cooks! We could have dinner so we can finish catching up. What do you think?

J: I never refuse good food! What kind of food are we having?

C: Mexican. My place; my dad will cook!

J: Sounds great! Mexican is my favorite. See you there.

C: See you.

2 **Now, imagine they are having dinner at Camila's house. Complete their conversation with the questions for the answers.**

1. **C:** So, Julia, tell me, ______________________________?

   J: On my last vacation, I went to Romania and Luxembourg.

2. **C:** ______________________________?

   J: I think Romania is more beautiful than Luxembourg.

3. **C:** ______________________________?

   J: The most important thing for me when traveling is getting in touch with locals.

LANGUAGE HELP

I like… (a lot / a little).
I love…
I enjoy…
I dislike…
I don't like…
I hate…
Do you like…?
So do I.
Me too.
Do you?
I don't.
What kind of… do you like?

3 **Now talk to a partner about things you like or don't like when on vacation. You can use some of the language in the Language Help box.**

Linked Skills

1 **Listen to this radio ad and check the activities mentioned in it.**

20

1.  ☐

4.  ☐

2.  ☐

5.  ☐

3.  ☐

6.  ☐

2 **Answer the questions about the ad.**

1. What is the ad about?

____

2. The ad gives an idea of familiarity with the customer. What elements of the text express this idea?

____

____

3. The ad tries to show that the company has a tradition in business but that it is also up to date with new technologies. Which part of the ad expresses this?

____

4. Mention one of the new technologies the company is using to help its customers.

____

____

World links

Career

Top 10 Jobs in Hospitality

by Rachel Zupek, CareerBuilder.com writer

21

[...] The hospitality industry, including but not limited to hotels, restaurants and meeting venues, is growing exponentially.

According to the U.S. Bureau of Labor Statistics, 12.4 million people work in the hospitality industry today, making about 8.6 percent of all employment. The hospitality industry is predicted to grow 17 percent between 2004 and 2014, adding more than 2.2 million new jobs to the work force. [...]

If you're looking for a job in an industry with continued job growth, here are [...] jobs to try your hand at:

1 Hotel general manager

Responsibilities: Directs everything involved in the operation and financial result of the property; creates standards for personnel administration and performance, service to patrons, room rates, advertising, publicity and food selection. [...]

2 Hotel clerk

Responsibilities: Performs an assortment of services for hotel guests, such as guest check-in and check-out, assigning rooms and answering inquiries to hotel services. [...]

3 Bellhop

Responsibilities: Escorts incoming hotel guests to rooms; assists with luggage; offers information about available services and facilities of hotel and entertainment attractions; inspects guest's room to make sure things are satisfactory. [...]

4 Meeting and convention planner

Responsibilities: Plans meetings and special events of various sizes. Coordinates such logistics as budgets, speakers, entertainment, transportation, facilities, technology, equipment, logistical requirements, printing, food and beverage, and other related issues. [...]

5 Concierge

Responsibilities: Assists guests with everything from making restaurant reservations to acquiring tickets to special events to helping with travel arrangements and tours of interesting places to visit. [...]

9 Maids and housekeeping cleaner

Responsibilities: Such light cleaning duties as making beds, replenishing linens, cleaning rooms and halls, vacuuming, emptying wastebaskets and restocking bathroom supplies. [...]

Rachel Zupek is a writer and blogger for CareerBuilder.com. She researches and writes about job search strategy, career management, hiring trends and workplace issues.

8 Reservation ticket agent

Responsibilities: Answers phone or e-mail inquiries; offers suggestions and information about travel arrangements, such as schedules, rates and types of accommodation; quotes fares and room rates; makes and confirms transportation and hotel reservations. [...]

7 Executive chef

Responsibilities: Oversees all kitchen activity, such as menu creation and staff management; utilizes food surpluses and leftovers; tracks popularity of various dishes; estimates customer food consumption; tests cooked foods by tasting and smelling them; creates special dishes and recipes. [...]

6 Maitre d'

Responsibilities: Also known as the head waiter, the maitre d' assigns customers to tables; makes advance reservations; oversees all aspects of the dining room experience for patrons; makes sure all waiters are doing their jobs effectively. [...]

Extracted from: http://www.careerbuilder.com/Article/CB-775-Who-is-Hiring-Top-10--Jobs-in-Hospitality/

World links

Reading Comprehension

1 **Read the text and complete the sentences with the job of the person.**

1. ______________________ is responsible, among other things, for the financial results.
2. ______________________ is responsible for helping guests with needs outside the hotel.
3. ______________________ are responsible for the cleanliness of guest rooms.
4. ______________________ is responsible for carrying the guests' luggage to their rooms.
5. ______________________ supervises all kitchen activities.
6. ______________________ is responsible for a variety of tasks related to guests' needs.

2 **Answer the questions.**

1. The correct translation for *patron* in topic 1 is ...

   a. patrão ☐ b. parente ☐ c. patrocinador ☐ d. freguês ☐

2. A synonym for *variety* that can be found in topic 2 is ______________________.
3. Check the activities that a bellhop does.

   a. Abrir a porta ☐

   b. Verificar e ajudar a garantir a satisfação do cliente com os quartos ☐

   c. Carregar bagagem ☐

   d. Fazer reservas em restaurantes ☐

   e. Ajudar na limpeza dos aposentos ☐

4. *Acquiring* in topic 5 is the same as...

   a. lending. ☐ b. buying. ☐ c. borrowing. ☐ d. reserving. ☐

5. The best translation for *oversees* in topic 7 is...

   a. rever. ☐ b. administrar. ☐ c. inspecionar. ☐ d. observar. ☐

6. The words for "excedentes" and "sobras" in topic 7 are ______________________ and ______________________.
7. A synonym for *questions* that can be found in topics 2 and 8 is ______________________.
8. The antonym of *filling up* that can be found in topic 9 is ______________________.
9. *Replenishing* in topic 9 means...

   a. repor. ☐ b. realocar. ☐ c. preencher. ☐ d. encher. ☐

3 **If you were to choose one of these jobs, which one would you go for? Why?**

____

____

Hyperlinks

air + energy

LINK 6

LOG IN

1 Where does most energy in Brazil come from?

2 Which sources of energy are more environmentally friendly?

WORD BANK

blades: lâminas
plains: planícies
shaft: eixo
shorelines: litoral, beira-mar
uneven: desigual

NOTES

Wind Basics

Wind is simply air in motion. It is caused by the uneven heating of the Earth's surface by the Sun. Because the Earth's surface is made of very different types of land and water, it absorbs the Sun's heat at different rates. One example of this uneven heating can be found in the daily wind cycle.

> Energy is power that is used to provide heat, operate machines etc.
>
> [Extracted from the *Longman Dictionary of Contemporary English.*]

How Uneven Heating of Water and Land Causes Wind

During the day, the air above the land heats up more quickly than the air over water. The warm air over the land expands and rises, and the heavier, cooler air rushes in to take its place, creating wind. At night, the winds are reversed because the air cools more rapidly over land than over water.

In the same way, the atmospheric winds that circle the Earth are created because the land near the Earth's equator is heated more by the Sun than the land near the North and South Poles.

Electricity Generation from Wind

Like old fashioned windmills, today's wind machines (also called wind turbines) use blades to collect the wind's kinetic energy. The wind flows over the blades creating lift, like the effect on airplane wings, which causes them to turn. The blades are connected to a drive shaft that turns an electric generator to produce electricity.

In 2011, wind turbines in the United States generated about 3% of total U.S. electricity generation. Although this is a small fraction of the Nation's total electricity production, it was equal to the annual electricity use of about 10 million households.

Where Wind is Harnessed

Operating a wind power plant is not as simple as just building a windmill in a windy place. Wind plant owners must carefully plan where to locate their machines. It is important to consider how fast and how much the wind blows at the site.

Wind power plants, or wind farms, as they are sometimes called, are clusters of wind machines used to produce electricity. A wind farm usually has dozens of wind machines scattered over a large area. The world's largest wind farm, the Horse Hollow Wind Energy Center in Texas, has 421 wind turbines that generate enough electricity to power 220,000 homes per year.

What about in Brazil?

Brazil's Electricity Generation by Source, 2010.

Source: EIA, International Energy Statistics

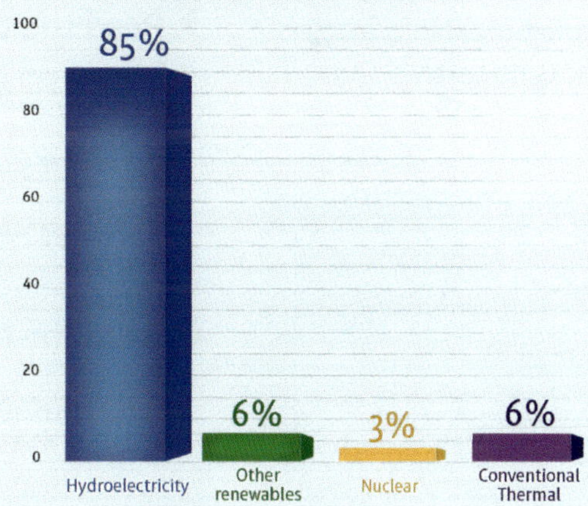

Extracted from: www.eia.gov/kids/energy.cfm?page=wind_home-basics-k.cfm

UNCOVERING THE *TEXT*

TOPIC

____

GENRE

What kinds of texts are the ones on pages 62 and 63?

- [ ] interview
- [ ] speech
- [ ] article
- [ ] graph

Dividing the text is a reading strategy!

Geralmente os textos já estão divididos em partes. Compreender ou fazer essa divisão temática ajuda a compreender cada segmento do texto, facilitando as coisas nos momentos em que seja necessário buscar informações específicas no texto.

RELATED LINKS

For more information on this Link's topics, please visit:

http://www.altenergy.org/
http://howtowritewhatever.com/how-to-write-an-invitation

FORUM

Looking at the graph on page 63, what can you infer about Brazil's electricity generation and what is the role of renewable energy sources, such as wind, in our country?

1 Skim the text and insert the subtitles in the correct place.

1. Wind Power Plants Produce Electricity
2. Wind Production
3. Energy from Moving Air
4. How Wind Turbines Work
5. Wind Power Plants Require Careful Planning
6. The Daily Wind Cycle

2 Scan the text and match the information.

1. Wind turbines in the United States in 2011
2. In the USA, 3% of total electricity represents the annual electricity use
3. Horse Hollow Wind Energy Center in Texas

- [ ] of about 10 million households.
- [ ] generated about 3% of total U.S. electricity.
- [ ] has 421 wind turbines.

3 Read the text and answer the questions.

1. How is wind defined in the text? ______________________
2. What's another name for wind power plants? ______________________
3. Where is the largest wind farm? ______________________

4 Read the text and then number the steps in the correct order.

- [ ] Then the wind causes lift (similar to airplane wings).
- [ ] The wind flows over the blades of the wind machines.
- [ ] The generator produces energy.
- [ ] When the blades turn, the drive shaft that is connected to them turns an electric generator.
- [ ] The blades turn.

5 According to the graph, what is the most important source of electricity in Brazil?

____

EXPANDING THE *VOCABULARY*

1 Underline all the cognates in the text below.

In 2009, most of the wind power plants in the world were located in Europe and in the United States, where government programs have helped support wind power development. The United States ranked first in the world in wind power generation, followed by Germany, Spain, China, and India. Denmark ranked ninth in the world in wind power generation, but generated about 19 percent of its electricity from wind, the largest share of any country.

2 The word *plant* in "Operating a wind power plant is not as simple as just building a windmill in a windy place" is a "false friend." Check its correct meaning and also the other underlined false friends.

1. Plant
   a. planta ☐ b. fábrica ☐ c. plano ☐
2. Companies must follow the rules when it comes to taxes.
   a. impostos ☐ b. taxas ☐ c. rendas ☐
3. Wind farms are usually very large.
   a. grande ☐ b. largo ☐ c. longo ☐
4. It was advised that students should carefully read the rules of the contest.
   a. com texto ☐ b. concurso ☐ c. contexto ☐
5. Government programs have helped support wind power development.
   a. suportar ☐ b. segurar ☐ c. sustentar ☐

3 Complete the paragraph with the prepositions from the box.

during from of over by

We can get a lot of energy ______________ the wind. The wind is caused ______________ the uneven heating ______________ the Earth's surface. The warm air ______________ the land expands and rises, and cool air substitutes it, creating winds. ______________ the night, we have the opposite process.

4 Use the correct word from the box to complete the questions.

energy	energetic	energize	energetically

1. What do you do when you want to feel more ______________________?
2. What are the most common sources of ______________________ in your country?
3. What do you enjoy doing more ______________________?
4. How do you ______________________ yourself after a long day at school?

5 Match the words that are similar in meaning.

1. heat up ☐ generate
2. motion ☐ movement
3. enough ☐ sufficient
4. create ☐ quickly
5. rapidly ☐ to warm up

6 Rewrite the phrases. Follow the example.

1. A source of energy is ______ *an energy source* ______.
2. Winds in the atmosphere are ______________________.
3. Energy that renews is ______________________.

7 Match the meanings of *plant* in the sentences.

1. It's the wrong time of year for planting roses.
2. He had planted the idea in the minds of the students.
3. Some workers don't want to move to the new plant.
4. I planted my chair beside hers.
5. Green plants obtain most of their energy from sunlight.

☐ set into the ground
☐ place firmly
☐ introduce into someone's mind
☐ factory
☐ living organism

DISCOVERING *GRAMMAR*

Passive Voice

These private companies *are known* as Independent Power Producers.
It *is caused* by the uneven heating.

A voz passiva é usada quando não sabemos, não queremos ou não precisamos mencionar quem faz a ação: The money *was stolen*. The bus *is being repaired*.

Se necessário, podemos mencionar quem fez a ação por meio da preposição *by*:

This book *was written* by the students.

Form: *to be* + verbo no *Past Participle*

Verb Tense	Active Voice	Passive Voice
Simple Present	takes can take	is/are taken can be taken
Simple Past	took could take	was/were taken could be taken
Present Continuous	is/are taking	is/are being taken
Past Continuous	was/were taking	was/were being taken
Present Perfect	has/have taken	has/have been taken
Past Perfect	had taken	had been taken
Future	will take	will be taken
Conditional	would take	would be taken

1 Fill in the blanks with the Passive Voice.

1. We will redecorate the apartment in July.
   The apartment ______________________________ in July.
2. He posted the letter last Friday.
   The letter ______________________________ last Friday.
3. She had spilled some tea on the carpet.
   Some tea ______________________________ on the carpet.

2 Rewrite the sentences in the Passive Voice.

1. We can sort out this problem. ______________________________
2. Somebody was cooking dinner when I got there. ______________________________
____
3. Have you moved the furniture? ______________________________

Writing an invitation

1 **Read the following paragraph and answer the questions.**

23

Welcome!
We invite you to gather in beautiful downtown Louisville with top researchers from Kentucky universities and industries to discuss the latest developments and challenges in renewable energy and energy efficiency technologies. Discover current research across the state and discuss a focused technological road map for commercialization of various renewable energy innovations in Kentucky. Excellent networking opportunity!

Extracted from: www.uoflalumni.org/s/1157/internal-3column.aspx?sid=1157&gid=1&pgid=1130&cid=2092&ecid=2092&ciid=4160&crid=0

1. What kind of paragraph is this?
   a. It's an academic paper. ☐
   b. It's an article. ☐
   c. It's an invitation. ☐
   d. It's a conversation. ☐
2. What kind of activity is going to happen in Kentucky?
   a. An academic event. ☐
   b. A party. ☐
   c. A ball. ☐
   d. A sales event. ☐
3. What is this event about?

____

2 **Based on the information you have so far about renewable energy and how electricity is used in your school, think of a name for an event about this subject.**

____

3 **Based on exercise 1 and using the name you created, make an invitation for your event. Remember to explain what it is about and why people should participate.**

Review

1 Check the alternative that has the correct answers to fill in all the blanks.

Adam bought a new car. It is ______________________ than his old one, but it isn't ______________________. In fact, it is much ______________________.

1. more quiet / bigger / smaller ☐
2. quieter / bigger / more small ☐
3. quieter / more big / smaller ☐
4. more quiet / more big / more small ☐
5. quieter / bigger / smaller ☐

2 Check the alternatives that have the correct comparative and superlative forms.

1. bad / badder / the baddest ☐
2. comfortable / comfortable / the comfortablest ☐
3. pretty / prettier / the prettiest ☐
4. far / farther / the farthest ☐
5. slowly / slowlier / the slowliest ☐

3 Check the alternative that has the correct answers to fill in the blanks.

She was one of ______________________ in the school.

These sandwiches are ______________________ than the ones at Big Burger.

1. the prettiest girls / the tastiest ☐
2. the prettiest girls / tastier ☐
3. the prettier girl / the tastier ☐
4. the prettiest girl / the tastiest ☐
5. the prettiest girl / tastier ☐

4 Check the sentence that is grammatically incorrect.

1. Damian is slightly shorter than his brother. ☐
2. I don't understand why they lost the game. They were by far the best players. ☐
3. Kelly prepared the most nice poster. Everybody liked it. ☐
4. These turbines are the fastest ever. ☐

5 **Check the alternative that shows the passive form of the sentence "He gave Mel a brand new iPod."**

1. A brand new iPod was gave to Mel. ☐
2. Mel was given a brand new iPod. ☐
3. He was given a brand new iPod by him. ☐
4. A brand new iPod is given by Mel. ☐
5. He was given a brand new iPod by Mel. ☐

6 **Fill in the blanks with the correct passive form.**

1. That tree ______________________ (plant) yesterday by my grandfather.
2. She ______________________ (drive) to the party last weekend by her father.
3. Renewable energy ______________________ (produce) by the new wind plant in Fortaleza since 2012.
4. The answers to the test can ______________________ (find) on the Internet two weeks after the exam.
5. They ______________________ (tell) to be quiet.
6. She ______________________ (advise) not to give her personal information to people without credentials.

7 **Rewrite the sentences in the passive form.**

1. Ole Kirk Christiansen invented LEGO in the late 1940s.

   ____

2. My parents bought a huge Christmas tree.

   ____

3. Carmen gave me a really beautiful bracelet on my birthday.

   ____

4. The atomic bomb destroyed Hiroshima.

   ____

5. The grasshoppers ate the whole plantation.

   ____

6. She received the news in awe.

   ____

8 **Read the text and fill in the blanks with the correct words from the box. Remember to use the correct comparative or superlative form.**

old unusual cool hot comfortable

One of the [1] ______________________ hotels I have ever been to is The Gamirasu Cave Hotel in Turkey. The hotel used to be a monastic retreat and is about a thousand years old, which makes it one of the [2] ______________________ hotels I know of. Although it was built for monks, it is [3] ______________________ than many others I've been to. Even on the [4] ______________________ summer days its rooms are [5] ______________________ many so-called traditional hotels.

9 **Write three sentences comparing the pictures.**

____

____

____

____

____

____

So far, SO GOOD?

1 **Use the codes to decipher the sentences. Identify the grammar topic in each of them.**

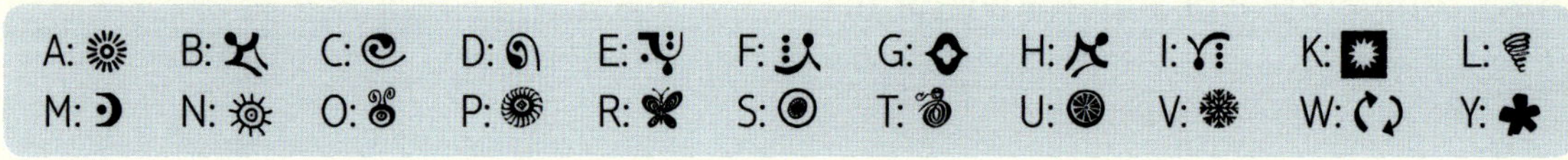

1. 

   ____

   Grammar topic: ______________

2. 

   ____

   Grammar topic: ______________

3. 

   ____

   Grammar topic: ______________

2 **Look at the sentences and guess.**

I. The heaviest aircraft to be pulled by a man weighed more than one hundred eighty tons.

II. The largest bubble gum bubble to be blown had a diameter of more than forty centimeters.

III. The longest nose on a living person measures almost nine centimeters.

Source: www.guinnessworldrecords.com/

1. All sentences are true. ☐
2. All sentences are false. ☐
3. Sentences I and II are true. ☐
4. Sentences II and III are true. ☐
5. Sentences I and III are true. ☐

Now that I've finished links 5 and 6, I can…

…compare people, places, and objects.	☐ Yes!	☐ I still need to study more!
…say and write about facts using the passive voice.	☐ Yes!	☐ I still need to study more!
…express my likes and dislikes.	☐ Yes!	☐ I still need to study more!
…write an invitation.	☐ Yes!	☐ I still need to study more!

Hyperlinks

culture + festivals

LINK 7

Parintins

Communication Bytes

Linked Skills

World Links

LINK 8

Afro-Brazilians

LINK 7

LOG IN

1 Which Brazilian festival do you like most?

2 Which festival, in your opinion, best represents Brazilian culture?

WORD BANK

be held: acontecer
chapel: capela
cruises: cruzeiros
fits: cabe, comporta
once upon a time: era uma vez
ox: boi
priest: padre
sponsors: patrocinadores
worldwide: mundialmente

NOTES

24 **Parintins**, *a city 230 miles from Manaus, hosts the Boi Bumbá folklore festival in late June, as significant as Carnaval in Rio in terms of colour and size. Two groups, Garantido (in red) and Caprichoso (in blue) compete inside an arena in front of 35,000 spectators: an unforgettable blend of drama, dance and music.*

Extracted from: Brochure of the Embassy of Brazil's tourist office; p.37

Shutterstock

[...]

The tradition says that, once upon a <u>time</u>, a pregnant woman wanted to eat the tongue of an ox; to satisfy her, the husband kills the most beloved ox in the farm. The priest of the village is called and says that the population must organize parties and celebrate feasts which, if happy enough, will bring the animal back to life.

Over the years, groups have been disputing which one can elaborate the most creative and artistic choreography to bring the animals back to life; with variations, the tradition of boi-bumbá (or bumba-meu-boi) is maintained in several Brazilian states.

[...]

An interesting rule is that, during the performance of one Ox, the adversaries must keep absolute silence; any negative manifestation may cause penalties. Also, all sponsors must give equal support to both groups; this caused the uncanny situation of Coca-Cola having to produce a version of its worldwide recognized red logo in a blue color, only to appear beside the Blue Ox. [...]

Extracted from: www.v-brazil.com/tourism/amazonas/parintins.html

UNCOVERING THE *TEXT*

TOPIC

___

GENRE

What kind of texts are the ones on pages 74 and 75?

- [ ] biography
- [ ] interview
- [ ] brochure
- [ ] article

Scanning is a reading strategy!

Examinar o texto minuciosamente, à procura de detalhes, ajuda a compreendê--lo num nível mais profundo.

RELATED LINKS

For more information on this Link's topics, please visit:

http://www.boibumba.com/
http://visual.ly/weird-and-wonderful-festivals-around-world

FORUM

What is the importance of festivals for a country?

1 Which alternative best describes the first text?

1. It tries to persuade the reader into doing something. [ ]
2. It describes the details of the festival. [ ]
3. It gives instructions about what to do at the festival. [ ]
4. It gives the reader facts about the festival in Parintins. [ ]

2 The tradition of "boi-bumbá" is part of Brazilian folklore, and there are tales about it. Which phrase in one of the texts is usually used when telling fairy tales or stories?

___

3 Scan the text and find...

1. **the distance of Parintins from Manaus:** ___
2. the number of groups that compete during the festival: ___
3. the number of people that fit in the Bumbódromo: ___
4. the colors of the two competing teams: ___
5. the company that changed the color of its logo because of the festival: ___

4 Which information is not given in the text?

1. The festival started with migrants during the rubber cycle. [ ]
2. There were several deaths during the first years of the festival. [ ]
3. Boi-bumbá in Parintins is a mega event. [ ]
4. The organization of the event is controlled by the Church. [ ]
5. At least one big company takes part by sponsoring the event. [ ]

EXPANDING THE *VOCABULARY*

1 Find synonyms in the text for the following words.

1. Parties, celebrations: ________________
2. A woman who carries a baby inside her body: ________________
3. A movable muscle inside your mouth: ________________
4. Viewers: ________________

2 Choose the best alternative.

1. ...**bring** the animal **back to life**

   a. ressuscitar ☐ b. nascer novamente ☐
2. A city 230 miles from Manaus **hosts** the Boi Bumbá folklore festival.

   a. hospedar ☐ b. organizar eventos ☐
3. An unforgettable **blend** of drama, dance, and music.

   a. mistura ☐ b. mudança ☐

3 Choose one of the underlined words from the text to complete all the sentences in each item.

1. It's ________________ for lunch!

   I don't have ________________ to study for the test today.

   ________________ me please, I'm sure this will be my fastest lap.
2. The ______________ was very uncomfortable in that bedroom.

   Many bacteria use insects as a ______________ and then, through the insects, reach human beings.

   Brazil will ________________ the Olympic Games in 2016.
3. I'm sorry, I'm ________________. Traffic was horrible today.

   We'll go to France in ________________ November.

   The ________________ president was honored for his deeds, even ten years after he died.

4 Match the words to their synonyms or definitions.

1. penalties	☐ strange; mysterious
2. performance	☐ fine; punishment
3. uncanny	☐ exhibition; representation
4. adversaries	☐ somebody you're opposed to

5 **In the text we find the word *unforgettable*, which has both a prefix and a suffix. Circle the suffixes and prefixes in each word below and match the words to their definition.**

1. unforgettable
2. unpredictable
3. disrespectful
4. unacceptable
5. unreliable

☐ something you can't allow, admit
☐ something or someone you will always remember
☐ that can't be trusted
☐ showing no appreciation
☐ something you can't foresee

6 **The words *worldwide* and *folklore* are both compound nouns. Use the available words from each side of the table to create other compound nouns and use them to complete the sentences.**

Compound Nouns

Substantivos compostos são formados pela combinação de duas palavras que têm cada uma seu significado quando separadas e que assumem um novo quando combinadas. Essas combinações variam, e entre elas podemos encontrar combinações de substantivo + substantivo; adjetivo + substantivo; adjetivo + verbo; verbo + substantivo; etc. No texto, temos *worldwide* (*world* + *wide*) e *folklore* (*folk* + *lore*).

bed	ball
week	board
birth	light
news	day
foot	end
key	paper
sun	room

1. Steve likes reading the ______________________ in the morning, after breakfast.
2. When I was a kid, I used to play ____________ all the time, until one day I had a problem with my knee and couldn't play anymore.
3. I try to keep my ____________ organized, but it's suddenly all messy. I don't know what happens.
4. Although tablets are great, I miss typing on the ____________.
5. People must expose themselves to ______________ a bit because it helps our body to stay healthy.
6. His parents will travel to Calgary on the ______________. They'll be back on Monday.
7. Her ____________ was yesterday. She's sixteen now.

DISCOVERING GRAMMAR

Conditional Sentences

The population must organize parties and celebrate feasts which, *if* happy enough, will bring the animal back to life.

A oração condicional vem ligada a uma oração principal (*main clause*) e pode expressar:

1. ordens, verdades universais, leis naturais (zero conditional)

   If the temperature falls below zero, water freezes.

2. ação/situação passível de acontecer (first conditional)

   If you eat too much, you will get a stomachache.

3. ação/situação imaginária ou improvável (second conditional)

   If I won the lottery, I would buy a new house.

4. ação/situação que era possível no passado, mas que agora é impossível de acontecer (third conditional)

   If I had worked hard, I would have passed the exam.

Form:

	if clause	**main clause**	
zero	Simple Present	Imperative or Simple Present	If it rains, take a taxi. If you add oil to water, the oil floats.
1st	Simple Present	*will* + verb	If he calls me, we'll go to the zoo.
2nd	Simple Past	*would* + verb	If he called me, we would go to the zoo.
3rd	Past Perfect	*would have* + Past Participle	If he had called me, we would have gone to the zoo.

Note: Conditional Tenses

Conditional

would + verbo: I would work if ... (Eu trabalharia se...)

Conditional Perfect

would have + verbo no particípio passado: I would have worked if... (Eu teria trabalhado se...)

1 Complete the sentences. Use the verbs in parentheses.

1. We ______________________ (go) to the beach if it is sunny.
2. If she passes her exams, she ______________________ (go) on vacation.
3. If she could swim, she ______________________ (go) to the club.
4. ______________________ (help) Tom if you could?
5. I ______________________ (help) her if she had asked.

Communication Bytes

1 **Dennis is thinking of going to Parintins to see the famous festival. Listen to his conversation with a hotel receptionist.** (25)

2 **What kind of festivals or holidays would you like to attend? Rank them from 1 (most interesting) to 5 (least interesting).**

1 

Boi-bumbá, Parintins, Amazonas ☐

2 

Carnaval, Rio de Janeiro, Rio de Janeiro ☐

3 

Carnaval, Salvador, Bahia ☐

4 

Gramado Film Festival, Gramado, Rio Grande do Sul ☐

5 

New Year's Eve at Paulista Avenue, São Paulo, São Paulo ☐

3 **Now work with a partner and pretend you want to go to one of the festivals from exercise 2 and your friend is the travel agent. You can use the language in the box.**

LANGUAGE HELP

Making requests	Responding to requests
Can you…., please?	Sure, here you are.
Will you…, please?	OK.
Could you possibly…, please?	No, I'm sorry…
Would you help me with…, please?	I'm afraid I can't.
Would you mind …ing, please?	

Linked Skills

1 **Listen to the following conversation and answer the question.**

26

1. What kind of conversation is this? Justify your choice.
   a. an informal talk between friends. ☐
   b. an interview. ☐
   c. a formal talk at the workplace. ☐

____

____

2 **Thinking about festivals such as the one in Parintins or Carnaval, what kind of picture do they paint of Brazil for foreigners? Debate this topic with your friends.**

3 **If you were to choose a festival to represent Brazil abroad, which one would it be and why? You can imagine a new one if necessary.**

____

____

____

____

____

____

____

____

____

Festivals Around the WORLD

27

SONGKRAN WATER FESTIVAL, THAILAND

The Thais celebrate Songkran, the Thai New Year, in mid-April, by visiting temples and family members, and throwing water.

The Thai New Year festival, one of the most exciting events in Thailand, is celebrated in the hottest month of the year. Young and grown-ups alike enjoy getting soaked and throwing water on anything that moves. [...]

Extracted from: http://suite101.com/article/songkran-new-year-water-festival-in-thailand-a223637

THE FALLAS, VALENCIA, SPAIN

The Fallas are enormous models made out of papier mache, wood and wax, and often caricaturing Spanish social and political current affairs. The models are burnt on the night of 19th March in a festival of fire, fireworks and organized mayhem. Fireworks and firecrackers play a big role in any fiestas held in this region, and Fallas is no exception. [...]

There are various theories concerning the origins of Fallas. Some claim that the festivals have been celebrated in Valencia since the Middle Ages when carpenters used to light a bonfire on 19th March, St Joseph Day. [...]

A second theory suggests that the tradition of lighting bonfires in honor of the saints arose from pagan customs which the Church accepted and adapted to its own interests, because their popularity made them impossible to ban.

Extracted from: http://www.euroresidentes.com/Fiestas/fallas.htm

JUNKANOO, NASSAU, BAHAMAS

Should your calendar permit, experience the Junkanoo cultural festival on Boxing Day (December 26) and New Year's Day. The origin of the word is obscure. Some say it comes from the French "L'inconnu", meaning the "unknown", in reference to the masks worn by the paraders. Others claim it is a dialectical adaptation for "John Canoe", the name of an African tribal chief who demanded the right to celebrate with his people even after being brought to the West Indies in slavery.

Slaves were given a special holiday from plantations at Christmas time, to be with family and celebrate with African dance, music, costumes and call on the spirit of the ancestors while giving themselves over to joyful exuberance. Today, Junkanoo has evolved to a more organized parade with intricate costumes, themed music and prizes.[...]

Extracted from: http://www.bahamasgo.com/treasures/junkanoo.htm

Reading Comprehension

1 Skim the texts and answer the questions.

1. What do the three texts have in common? ______________________________
2. Which festival celebrates the New Year? ______________________________
3. Which festival is of slave origin? ______________________________
4. Which festival may have its origin in the Middle Ages? ______________________________

2 Match the information to the festival.

New Year · papier mache · ancestors · April · slavery · Thailand · Spain · water · temples · family · political · fireworks · Bahamas · Christmas · Middle Ages · bonfire · masks

Songkran	Junkanoo	Fallas

3 Read the text about Songkran and complete the information.

1. The Thai New Year is celebrated in ______________________________.
2. They enjoy themselves by ______________________________.

4 Choose the best translation for the words below (taken from text 2).

1. current affairs	☐ confusão
2. mayhem	☐ bombinha (fogo de artifício)
3. firecrackers	☐ dizem
4. claim	☐ atualidades

5 Explain in your own words the meaning of the expressions taken from the text about Junkanoo.

1. demanded the right (line 7): ______________________________
2 giving themselves over (line 12): ______________________________
3. joyful exuberance (line 12): ______________________________
4. themed music (line 14): ______________________________

Hyperlinks

culture + festivals

LINK 8

LOG IN

1 How many different nationalities is Brazil made of?

2 What do you know about your ancestors?

WORD BANK

drums: tambores
pork: carne de porco
slaves: escravos
slavery: escravatura
strength: força

NOTES

Afro-Brazilian

History, Beats, and Culture

[...] Today Brazil has the largest population of Black origin outside of Africa, estimated at 90 million people.

Starting around 1550, the Portuguese began trading slaves from the West African and Central African regions of Ghana, Benin, Nigeria, Angola, Congo, and [Southeast Africa] Mozambique. An estimated four million people, thirty seven percent of all the captured Africans forced into slavery, were settled in Brazil to work in the sugar plantations and mining industry. Slavery was the foundation of the Brazilian economy until 1888, when slavery was legally abolished.

As with all great migrations, the Africans that arrived in Brazil not only brought over their strength and beauty but also their music and cultural traditions. Their cultural traditions would inevitably blend with the Portuguese and Amerindian customs, to produce a unique cultural manifestation of its own.

Lauri Lyons is the author of Flag: *An American Story and Flag International*

Extracted from: www.huffingtonpost.com/lauri-lyons/afro-brazilian-history-be_b_452877.html

The Afro-Brazilian Culture

29

Samba was one of the first expressions of the Afro-Brazilian culture to be admired, and it has occupied a distinguished position in the popular music. However, the African drums have also brought something other than chants and dances with them. Besides the samba, the African influence on Brazilian music goes from the Maracatu to the Congada, Cavalhada and Mozambique, sounds and rhythms that travel and conquer Brazil from end to end.

A martial art developed for defensive purposes, the Capoeira was taught to the captive Africans by slaves who were captured and returned to the mills. In order not to raise any suspicions, the fight movements were adapted to look like dancing under the sound of African chants. Capoeira was prohibited for many decades in Brazil. The practice remained illegal until the 1930s, when a variation (more as a sport than a cultural manifestation), was presented to the President Getúlio Vargas.

During the slave trade period, the Africans were baptized on their arrival and forced to follow the Catholic religion.
However, in the majority of times, the conversion did not really occur, and the African religions continued being practiced in secret. [...]
The Afro-Brazilian religions constitute a relatively recent phenomenon in the Brazilian religious history. Candomblé, the most traditional and African among these religions, began in the Northeast. It began in the state of Bahia, and has been synonymous of Afro-Brazilian religions in general.

The African presence is outstanding and fundamental on Brazilian gastronomy, with dishes such as the vatapá, acarajé, caruru, mungunzá, sarapatel, baba de moça, cocada, coconut candy, and many others. Another very popular dish is the feijoada, which originates from the senzalas (slave quarters). [...]

UNCOVERING THE *TEXT*

TOPIC

____

GENRE

What kinds of text are on pages 86 and 87?

- [ ] article and biography
- [ ] article and timeline
- [ ] novel and synopsis
- [ ] articles

Skimming is a reading strategy!

Ao passarmos os olhos sobre um texto, podemos encontrar informações específicas sem precisar de todos os detalhes.

RELATED LINKS

For more information on this Link's topics, please visit:

http://afrobrazilianincubator.org/
http://slaveryfootprint.org

FORUM

The texts show that the presence of Africans in Brazil has influenced its culture and traditions, enriching them and being part of our national identity. Still, even nowadays, there are demonstrations of prejudice based on color or ethnic background. What can be done to change that?

1 **Do the authors of the texts express their opinions?**

____

2 **Why can we say that the texts are impartial?**

____

3 **Skim the first text and say what the numbers refer to.**

1. 90,000,000 ______________________
2. 1550 ______________________
3. 4,000,000 ______________________
4. 37 ______________________
5. 1888 ______________________

4 **Read each topic of the second text carefully and then choose a title for each of them.**

1. Cuisine 2. Religion 3. Music 4. Capoeira

5 **Choose the correct option.**

1. The first text is about the history of Afro descendants in Brazil, the second is about how the influence of African culture can be seen in Brazil.
2. The first text states the different cultures didn't blend in Brazil.
3. The second text presents areas which the African culture had an influence.

a. All the sentences are correct. ☐
b. Sentences 1 and 3 are correct. ☐
c. Sentences 2 and 3 are correct. ☐
d. Only sentence 1 is correct. ☐

EXPANDING THE *VOCABULARY*

1 Read the text below and underline all the cognates.

The Afro-Brazilian religions constitute a relatively recent phenomenon in Brazilian religious history. Candomblé, the most traditional and African among these religions, began in the Northeast. It began in the state of Bahia and has been synonymous of Afro-Brazilian religions in general.

2 Read the texts and find the words that fit the definitions.

1. Extremely good or impressive: ______________________________
2. The food that remains at the end of a meal after you have finished eating: __________________
3. To mix different foods or other substances together: ______________________________
4. Food prepared and cooked in a particular way: ______________________________
5. People who have control over servants or other people who work for them: _________________
6. To continue to be in a particular situation or condition: ______________________________
7. Event when people change countries: ______________________________
8. Many people know and like it, so it is ______________________________.

3 In the sentence "An estimated four million people […] were settled in Brazil to work in the sugar plantations and mining industry," the verb *settled* means to find a permanent place to live. Look at the sentences and choose the best meaning for *settle* in each of them.

1. I don't want to fight anymore. Let's settle this and go on with our lives, please!
2. The baby wouldn't settle, so I gave her a pacifier. It helped a lot.
3. Well, I finally decided to settle in the countryside.
4. Have you settled on a place to have dinner? I'm hungry.
5. It's time you settle down and start saving some money for the future.
6. She wanted that perfume, but it is too expensive, so she settled for a cheaper one.

- [ ] to make a place your permanent home
- [ ] to start to have a quieter life
- [ ] to put an end to an argument
- [ ] to accept something that is less than expected
- [ ] to decide something
- [ ] to become or make someone calm

4 In exercise 3, there are three phrasal verbs. Identify and underline them.

____

5 Check the correct interpretation for each sentence.

1. The African presence is outstanding and fundamental in Brazilian gastronomy.
   a. Brazilian gastronomy has incorporated many elements of African gastronomy in a very good way. ☐
   b. African gastronomy is better than Brazilian gastronomy. ☐
2. Their cultural traditions would inevitably blend with the Portuguese and Amerindian customs, to produce a unique cultural manifestation of its own.
   a. African, Portuguese, and Amerindian cultures formed only one culture in Brazil. ☐
   b. The Afro-Brazilian culture is a mix of Portuguese, Amerindian, and African cultures. ☐
3. Today Brazil has the largest population of black origin outside of Africa.
   a. Many Africans come to Brazil every year. ☐
   b. Many people in Brazil are descended from Africans. ☐

6 In the sentence "A martial art developed for defensive purposes," the word *defensive* is an adjective meaning someone or something that can perform the action of defending. Add the suffix *-ive* to the following verbs and use them in the correct sentences.

1. instruct: ____________________
2. persuade: ____________________
3. compete: ____________________
4. protect: ____________________

a. She's a very ____________________ salesperson. That's why she receives such great comissions.
b. My parents are very ____________________ of my sister because she has some special needs.
c. Being ____________________ is not always good. Sometimes it's better just to have fun.
d. That's a very ____________________ manual. Now I know how to use my washing machine properly.

Suffixes

O sufixo *-ive* torna verbos em adjetivos que mostram a habilidade de alguém ou algo para fazer a ação indicada pelo verbo.

DISCOVERING GRAMMAR

Direct and Indirect Speech

Lauri Lyons said that Brazil has the largest population of black origin outside of Africa

Podemos usar o discurso direto (*direct speech*) ou o discurso indireto (*indirect speech*) para relatar o que alguém diz:

Lisa: Mom, I'm going to school.

Direct speech – Lisa said, "Mom, I'm going to school."

Indirect speech – Lisa said that she was going to school.

Quando passamos uma oração do discurso direto para o indireto, ocorrem alterações em verbos, expressões de tempo e algumas outras palavras. Observe:

Direct speech		Indirect speech
Imperative	→	**Infinitive**
"Open the door."		She told me to open the door.
Present		**Past**
"I'm from Spain."		She said (that) she was from Spain.
Present Continuous		**Past Continuous**
"I'm working."		She said she was working.
Future		**Conditional**
"I'll dance all night."		She said she would dance all night.
Simple Past / Present Perfect		**Past Perfect**
"I bought it."		She said she had bought it.
"I've arrived early."		She said she had arrived early.
Past Continuous		**Past Perfect Continuous**
"I was sleeping."		She said she had been sleeping.
Must		**Have to**
"You must be tolerant."		She said I had to be tolerant.
***Wh-* question**		**Indirect question**
"What time is it?		She asked me what time it was.

Outras mudanças: this – that / these – those / here – there / today – that day / yesterday – the day before / tomorrow – the following day

1 Check the correct form for the indirect speech.

1. Glenn: "How old is she?"
   a. Glenn asked how old was she? ☐
   b. Glenn asked how old she was. ☐
2. Tom: "You must arrive early."
   a. Tom said we had to arrive early. ☐
   b. Tom said we can arrive early. ☐
3. Peter: "Can you fix the computer?"
   a. Peter asked if I could fix the computer. ☐
   b. Peter said that we could fix the computer. ☐

Describing a person

1 **Read the following sentence from the third text again:**

> [...] A 45-year-old teacher, C. L. S., was arrested on Tuesday (October 23), suspected of a racial slur against a black SAMU (Serviço de Atendimento Móvel de Urgência, or Mobile Service Emergency Care) doctor in Juazeiro, (located in the northeastern state of) Bahia. [...]
>
> Extracted from: blackwomenofbrazil.co/2012/12/03/black-doctor-and-lawyer-discover-what-one-calls-a-negro-with-a-ph-d/

This sentence gives a brief description about two people. Write the information you have about them.

1. C. L. S.: ____________________
2. G. B. (his name appears only further into the news): ____________________

2 **Now, read this conversation between two friends and answer the question.**

N: So, Jules, guess what. I'm meeting that girl today!

J: What girl, Nick?

N: The one with that beautiful afro! Remember her?

J: Not really.

N: Come on, you've got to remember her. We met at Donna's party. She was wearing a flowered dress, golden necklace and earrings, about our age, eighteen tops. She had those thick lips, thin hands, about five feet tall, slim, dark eyes…

What details are there about her physical appearance?

____

3 **Imagine that a friend is coming to your city. Write a clear description about him/her so that your brother can pick your friend up at the airport. Follow the model and use the words from the box to help you.**

Age	Height	Body	Hair	Details	Clothes
old	tall	heavy	long	mole	jeans
young	medium	muscular	short	scar	shirt
thirty	short	thin	wavy	wrinkles	skirt
forty		skinny	straight	freckles	T-shirt
			curly	beard	sneakers
			dark	mustache	
			blonde	braces	
			light		

Review

1 Match the halves of the sentences to make complete ones.

1. If you are a qualified and reliable professional,
2. She would never eat raw fish again
3. If you study a foreign language,
4. If I could choose any country in the world,
5. This city will never be a better place
6. They will need to practice

- [ ] you will also learn about another culture.
- [ ] if they want to be good musicians.
- [ ] you will certainly get a promotion.
- [ ] I'd choose to live in Austria.
- [ ] if we don't put an end to violence.
- [ ] if she knew she would get sick.

2 Read the sentences and choose the correct alternative.

1. If you start exercising, you won't regret it.
2. There are all sorts of festivals all over the world.
3. Many people are unemployed nowadays.

a. A frase 1 está errada. [ ]

b. A expressão *there are* pode ser trocada por *have*. [ ]

c. O pronome *it* na frase 1 se refere a "exercitar-se". [ ]

d. A frase 3 diz que há muitas pessoas não qualificadas para trabalhar atualmente. [ ]

3 Check the alternative in which the following sentence is reported correctly.

Kevin said, "Marina was speaking on the phone."

1. Kevin said that Marina spoke on the phone. [ ]
2. Kevin said Marina had spoken on the phone. [ ]
3. Kevin said Marina had been speaking on the phone. [ ]

4 Choose the sentences that are grammatically correct.

1. Celia has been starting a diet. ☐
2. Diana was trying to put the baby to sleep when her friend called. ☐
3. She explained to him what they had done. ☐
4. If it rains heavily, the streets flood. ☐
5. If I would come, he would come too. ☐
6. If she has asked me, I would stay with her. ☐

5 Use the words from the box to form collocations.

absolute	do	hard	grant	early	water	answer	event	play	luck

1. perfumed ______________
2. ______________ morning
3. ______________ a prayer
4. ______________ a wish
5. mega ______________
6. ______________ silence
7. ______________ a musical instrument
8. ______________ crosswords
9. wish you ______________
10. study ______________

6 Check the incorrect alternative.

Max is a bachelor who lives in a small apartment in London. He enjoys eating, and he usually prepares his meals. His favorite hobby is cooking. He has practiced so much that he can be considered an expert cook.

1. Max is a cook. ☐
2. Cooking is his pastime. ☐
3. Max is not married. ☐

7 Rewrite the sentences using indirect speech.

1. What time does the game start?

   I asked her ____.

2. What are you going to do next?

   She asked me ____.

3. Don't forget to come early on Wednesday.

   She told me ____.

4. Please write to me.

   Bill asked Maria ____.

5. You can come and visit us any time.

   They invited ____.

8 Match the reported sentences to the original statements.

1. She said she had to go.
2. He promised he would bring some food.
3. She suggested we should write to the airline.
4. I insisted she should see the doctor.
5. He complained he was too tired.

- [ ] "You can't go on like this. Make an appointment with the doctor."
- [ ] "I'm afraid it's time for me to leave."
- [ ] "If I were you, I'd write to the airline."
- [ ] "I'll certainly bring some food."
- [ ] "I'm far too tired these days."

9 Complete the sentences with the appropriate verb in the Simple Past.

1. They ____________________ to us that we would have to wait. (explain / tell)
2. She ____________________ them they should reconsider their decision. (say / persuade)
3. He ____________________ that the prices had gone up. (answer / ask)
4. We ____________________ him we would be quiet. (say / tell)
5. He ____________________ to me that you were rude. (remind / complain)
6. She ____________________ us that she could not come. (inform / promise)
7. She ____________________ I have another slice. (insist / persuade)
8. He ____________________ he didn't know. (tell / say)
9. She ____________________ him to be quiet. (invite / warn)

So far, SO GOOD?

1 **Look at the picture and use your imagination to complete the sentences.**

1. If they find a ball, ____________________.
2. If a giant grizzly bear started chasing them, ____________________.
3. If they had been running away from a monster, ____________________.

2 **Cross out the odd word. Use a dictionary to help you when necessary.**

1. festival, feast, celebration, happiness, fete
2. church, chapel, abbey, minster, monastic
3. hill, mountain, house, peak, mount
4. wrist, ankle, calf, bag, knee
5. cruise, breeze, journey, crossing, sailing
6. cleric, priest, dean, father, vicar

Now that I've finished links 7 and 8, I can…

…talk about real and hypothetical conditions.	☐ Yes!	☐ I still need to study more!
…report what people say.	☐ Yes!	☐ I still need to study more!
…ask and answer questions using a variety of verb tenses.	☐ Yes!	☐ I still need to study more!
…write a description of someone.	☐ Yes!	☐ I still need to study more!

APPENDICES

UFMG 2010 fase 1

After Capitalism

The era of transition that we are entering will be disruptive – but it may bring a world where markets are servants, not masters.

To understand what capitalism might become, we first have to understand what it is. This is not so simple. Capitalism includes a market economy, but many traditional market economies are not capitalistic. It includes trade, but trade, too, long precedes capitalism. It includes capital – but Egyptian pharaohs and fascist dictators commanded surpluses too.

The French historian Fernand Braudel offered perhaps the best description of capitalism when he wrote of it as a series of layers built on top of the everyday market economy of onions and wood, plumbing and cooking. These layers, local, regional, national and global, are characterized by ever greater abstraction, until at the top sits disembodied finance, seeking returns anywhere, uncommitted to any particular place or industry, and commodifying anything and everything.

Only a few decades ago there was great interest in what would supersede capitalism. The answers ranged from communism to managerialism and from hopes of a golden age of leisure to dreams of a return to community and ecological harmony. Today these utopias can be found in the movements around the World Social Forum, on the edges of all of the major religions, in the radical sub-cultures that surround the net, and in moderated form in thousands of civic ventures across the world.

MULGAN, Geoff. Available at: http://www.prospect-magazine.co.uk/article_details.php?id=10680
Access on June 17th, 2009

1 The phrasal verb "tie in" (line 5) means:

a. guides transitions.

b. rules the world.

c. serves the market.

d. teaches governors.

2 The best topic for the first paragraph is that

a. capitalism includes market economy.

b. it is not very easy to define capitalism.

c. the elements in capitalism are traditional.

d. we cannot tell the future of capitalism.

3 The word disembodied (line 15) can be best understood as:

a. foreign.
b. marketed.
c. nearby.
d. vague.

UFSC 2012

Add the numbers of the **correct** statements and write the sum in the boxes at the end of each question.

TEXT 2

The Living Library

1. From the mid 40's to the 70's, many big cities in Brazil expanded because of internal migrations. During those years, with the intensification of social problems, many non-governmental organizations were created and many existing Community Centers increased their activities to provide non-formal education for children and adolescents after school hours.

2. The "Living Library" is a two-year project that aims at making the act of reading and writing as an everyday activity for poor children and their teachers. This would mean fewer failures in elementary school and more children learning about their reality and how to change it. These "libraries" are being implanted in Community Centers in charge of children and adolescents living in the poor districts of the peripheral area of the big cities, where huge slums and acute social problems are concentrated. To achieve its objective the Project team provides personal development for the community teachers by preparing them to work with books and reading activities in the context of poverty and deprivation of their institutions. Each library is unique, taking into account the needs and the culture of the community where it is located.

3. Forty-four institutions took part in the selective process. Among those, 10 were chosen to receive the library: two in Brasília and eight in São Paulo. Fourteen community teachers went through a 44 hour training program. The first 10 libraries received 4,000 books directly benefiting 2,500 children and adolescents.

4. The first 10 libraries were implanted and are open to the community. They attend institutions that look after street children from slums in the suburbs, children living in poor houses downtown, children living in shelters, who have no parents or are temporarily separated from them.

From: <http://www.unesco.org/most/southam7.htm>
Access on August 18, 2010. (Adapted)

4 **Select the CORRECT proposition(s), according to text 2.**

01. Internal migration is a phenomenon still happening in Brazil.

02. The activities developed by the "Living Library" happen during school hours.

04. Community teachers receive special training in order to work in the Project.

08. The "Living Library" is a project intended to exist permanently.

16. Children taking part in the Project have a chance to perform better at school.

32. Every "Library" pays special attention to the characteristics of its community.

64. Ten "Living Libraries" are located in community centers for homeless children.

☐

5 **Select the CORRECT proposition(s).**

Text 2 gives information about the "Living Library" project as for:

01. its cost

02. its objective

04. its director

08. its duration

16. its disadvantage

32. its location

☐

ESPM 2011

Facebook Tops 500 Million Users

By JENNA WORTHAM

Facebook, the social network created in the dormitories of Harvard six years ago, said on Wednesday that it now had 500 million members.

The company has doubled in size from a year ago, pushing international competitors aside.

"This is an important milestone for all of you who have helped spread Facebook around the world," Mark Zuckerberg, the company's 26-year-old chief executive, said in a company blog post.

Facebook's dizzying rise has not been without stumbles. Most recently, the company was the focus of intense scrutiny over changes to its site that encouraged members to make more information about themselves accessible to anyone on the Internet.

A recent survey by the American Customer Satisfaction Index showed that user satisfaction with Facebook stood at 64 on a 100-point scale, which placed it in the bottom 5 percent of the companies covered in the index.

Facebook's popularity has also spurred competition from the likes of Google, which views the billions of links and hours spent on the site each month as a threat to its business. But if anything, the site's steady growth in spite of its setbacks only validates the company's approach, said Ray Valdes, an analyst at the research firm Gartner.

Facebook has been aggressive in pushing users "to the edge of their comfort zone," Mr. Valdes said. "But Facebook has proven that it can weather those challenges and still grow."

Mr. Valdes, who estimates that Facebook is adding 50 million new members each month, attributed the company's rapid ascension to its continuous effort to change and improve the service.

"That keeps it bubbling away," he said.

(The New York Times, July 21, 2010)
Available at: www.poetry-archive.com/m/marlowe_christopher.html

6 The title "Facebook Tops 500 Million Users" most likely means that:

a. Facebook has almost 500 million users.
b. Facebook will soon have 500 million users.
c. Facebook has already reached the number of 500 million users.
d. Facebook shall surpass 500 million users in a near future.
e. Facebook excelled the number of 500 million users six years ago.

7 The important milestone Mark Zuckerberg refers to is:

a. The user's satisfaction with Facebook.
b. The company's astonishing profitability.
c. The number of users.
d. The qualified team that has helped to spread Facebook around the world.
e. The results of a recent survey by the American Customer

IME 2012

Choose the correct alternatives to complete the text.

Atmospheric Physics is the study of physical processes in the atmosphere; understanding the climate and the weather, and the physical reasons ____8____ it is as it is and how it might change in the future.

Getting Started Vestibular

My own particular research background is in radiative transfer and ___9___ I mean the transport of electromagnetic radiation through the atmosphere; ___10___ the Sun's radiation coming in, getting absorbed and scattered in the air, and the transfer of heat radiation emitted by the Earth's surface.

From a ___11___ physics perspective there's an awful lot of things about the atmosphere that we don't understand, and of course, it's very classical physics in the ___12___ that it's looking at fluid dynamics and thermodynamics applied to the natural environment. What motivates us really is to try and explain what we see in the environment, what ___13___ it and what might change it in the future, both in ___14___ of local weather but also climate, by ___15___ I mean larger areas and larger timescales.

My background has led me to an interest in how solar radiation ___16___ in the atmosphere, so ___17___ at how changes in the Sun might affect the climate for the past year.

8

a. as
b. because
c. for
d. why
e. that

9

a. these
b. as long as
c. as soon as
d. which
e. by that

10

a. both
b. neither
c. if
d. but
e. not only

11

a. purposely
b. possibly
c. purely
d. poorly
e. previously

12

a. away
b. sense
c. meaning
d. understand
e. definition

13

a. affections
b. cause
c. effects
d. affects
e. demands

14

a. units
b. reference
c. relation
d. conditions
e. terms

15

a. which
b. who
c. whom
d. whose
e. whether

16

a. absorbed
b. is absorbing
c. has absorbed
d. is absorbed
e. absorbs

17

a. I had looked
b. I've been looking
c. I look
d. I will look
e. I haven't looked

ANSWER KEY

UFMG 2010

1. C
2. B
3. D

UFSC 2012

4. 04+16+32 = 52
5. 02+08+32 = 42

ESPM 2011

6. C
7. C

IME 2012

8. D
9. E
10. A
11. C
12. B
13. D
14. E
15. A
16. D
17. B

Link 1

1 **Complete the sentences below with the Present Perfect tense.**

1. I ________________ (not find) what I am looking for.
2. ________________ your teacher ________________ (give) you the results?
3. Sarah and Jim ________________ (choose) their honeymoon destination.
4. Where ________________ (spend) your nights recently?
5. They ________________ (feel) a little embarrassed with the situation.
6. What ________________ the children ________________ (eat) today?

2 **Select the sentences that can be written in the Present Perfect Continuous without changing the meaning.**

1. Sheila has lived in Montreal for 5 years. ☐
2. They have arrived at home. ☐
3. Have you felt sick lately? ☐
4. Pietro hasn't spoken to Flavia for a stupid reason. ☐
5. I have given Robert some suggestions. ☐
6. Norton has lost his credit cards. ☐

Now, rewrite the ones you selected into the Present Perfect Continuous.

____

____

____

____

____

3 **Give the questions for the following answers.**

1. ____?

   Paul hasn't come to the meeting.

2. ____?

   No, I haven't seen your kid.

3. ____?

   My brother has gone to the market.

4. ____?

They have bought <u>a new car</u>.

5. ____?

I <u>have given</u> that old book away.

6. ____?

We have been to China <u>three times</u>.

4 The sentences below are *not* correct. Read and correct them.

1. My parents hasn't told me the true story. ______________________
2. Where you have gone? ______________________
3. Daniel has not sang my favorite song. ______________________
4. Tell me if you have cutted the meat. ______________________
5. Why haven't they came to the party? ______________________
6. The rain haven't stopped! ______________________

5 Put the verbs in the box in the correct columns according to the variation they have, starting with the base form column. Then complete the Simple Past and Past Participle form columns. Study the example.

put – buy – bring – send – keep – do – be – go – cut – set – quit – grow – feel – fall – bet

ONE FORM			TWO FORMS			THREE FORMS		
Base form	Past form	Past Participle form	Base form	Past form	Past Participle form	Base form	Past form	Past Participle form
put	*put*	*put*	*buy*	*bought*	*bought*	*be*	*was/were*	*been*

6 Answer the following questions.

1. Have you studied at other schools?

____

2. Have you been talking in English out of the classroom?

____

Link 2

1 **Complete the sentences using *for* or *since*.**

1. I have been waiting for you ______________ around two hours.
2. We have been here ______________ two o'clock.
3. I have lived in this neighborhood ______________ I was a child.
4. They have been in love ____________ 15 years, ____________ they met each other at school.
5. ______________ some weeks, I couldn't reach her. I think she has been sad ______________ her father passed away.

2 **Use the adverbs *since, ever, for, already, yet,* or *just* in each sentence.**

1. I haven't finished the activity ____________.
2. Have you ____________ talked to James? I thought he wasn't here.
3. Has Georgia ____________ eaten escargot?
4. They have discussed for hours, ____________, they haven't come to a conclusion.
5. We have ____________ seen Mary. She left a minute ago!
6. The kids have been playing ____________ early afternoon.
7. They have been working here ____________ some time now.

3 **You will find a problem in each of the sentences below. Read and correct them.**

1. When have you traveled to Cairo?

   ____

2. They have tried Indian food last weekend.

   ____

3. The Durians lived in this house since 2005.

   ____

4. Why haven't they arrived at 8 A.M. yesterday?

   ____

5. The students didn't start the exams yet.

   ____

4 **Write sentences using the words in parentheses and the Simple Past tense or the Present Perfect tense. Follow the example.**

1. She looks more beautiful. _Has she lost weight?_ (She / lose / weight / ?)
2. ______________________ (you / do / this / before / ?) Do you need assistance?
3. Is the room a mess again? ______________________ (the lady / clean / it) last week, John!
4. ______________________ (He / cut / himself) when he was cooking dinner.
5. ______________________ (I / not / speak) to Julian yet.
6. ______________________ (Frank / watch / that movie) twice, so far.

5 **Read the sentences below, identify the verb tenses used, and think about the differences between them. Discuss with your classmates and teacher.**

1. We studied English for 5 years. ______________________
2. We have studied English for 5 years. ______________________
3. Helen hasn't given her opinion yet. ______________________
4. Helen didn't give her opinion in the meeting. ______________________
5. Have you read this text? ______________________
6. Did you read this text? ______________________

6 **Check the correct statements about exercise 5.**

1. In sentence 1, the person is not studying anymore, but in sentence 2, the person is still studying. ☐
2. Sentences 3 and 4 have no difference in meaning. ☐
3. Sentence 5 is incorrect. ☐
4. The use of the Present Perfect and the adverb *yet* in sentence 3 shows Helen still has a chance to express her opinion. ☐

7 **Answer the question: Have you ever been abroad? Give a long and detailed answer.**

____

Link 3

1 **Match the sentences below.**

1. Before Greg arrived,
2. Jeff bought a new apartment because
3. My boss called me because
4. By the time the movie started,
5. When Bobby asked for the bill,

- [ ] I had already paid for everything.
- [ ] I had arrived late for work.
- [ ] his kids had already gone to bed.
- [ ] we had bought soda and popcorn.
- [ ] he had saved more money.

2 **Complete the sentences with the verbs in the box in the Past Perfect tense.**

leave - speak - arrive - get - fix - write

1. When she offered me some pills, I ____________ already ____________ some I found in the cabinet.
2. Her friends ____________ already ____________ when she got to the festival.
3. By the time I thought about asking the director, Juan ____________ to him.
4. The young musician ____________ that song before his teacher had the idea.
5. When I got to the store, the technician ____________ my notebook.
6. By the time the plane landed, my family ____________ at the airport to pick me up.

3 **Rewrite these sentences in the Past Perfect Continuous.**

1. The girls hadn't eaten much meat.

   ____

2. Who had called you?

   ____

3. Theo had listened to music all day long.

   ____

4. I had studied when you called.

   ____

5. The secretary hadn't answered her calls.

   ____

6. Leonard had argued with his friends.

   ____

4 **Write four questions for this sentence: "Marion had bought some gifts at that shop before you did." Use words such as *who*, *what*, and *where* to help you.**

____

____

____

____

5 **Complete the following conversations with the correct alternatives.**

1. A: Hey, what happened? I __________ for you!

   B: I stayed there for a long time, and then I left.

   A: So, when I __________, you __________ already __________ .

   a. was waiting / arrived / had left ☐

   b. waited / had arrived / left ☐

   c. was waiting / arrived / left ☐

2. A: __________ you ever __________ that movie?

   B: No, I __________ it yet.

   a. have saw / haven't saw ☐

   b. did see / didn't seen ☐

   c. have seen / haven't seen ☐

3. A: He __________ before I __________ him.

   B: That's why he __________ the phone.

   a. had gone to sleep / called / didn't answer ☐

   b. had slept / was calling / answers ☐

   c. was sleeping / was calling / was answering ☐

6 **Answer the questions.**

1. Had the teacher arrived when you entered the classroom?

   ____

2. Had your friends arrived at school by the time you got there?

   ____

3. What had you done in the afternoon by the time you got home last night?

   ____

Link 4

1 Underline the mistakes and correct the sentences below.

1. I am glad to saying I liked the results.
2. Avoid to go home late.
3. They can't stand take buses.
4. She promised calling me tomorrow.
5. Miguel invited me going to the movies.
6. The students mustn't to speak loud in class.

2 Circle the right form of the verbs in these sentences.

1. That knife is *to cut / cutting* chicken only.
2. I am not really interested in *to go / going* with them.
3. She kept *to think / thinking* about what I had said.
4. My father taught me how *to fish / fishing*.
5. He couldn't help *to fall / falling* in love with his classmate.
6. His sister was the second *to have / having* a suggestion for the meeting.

3 Choose a word from the box to complete the sentences. Use each word only ONCE.

dancing – to dance – telling – to tell – talking – to talk – stay – to stay – staying

1. My teacher keeps ____________ until the last minute.
2. I really enjoy ____________ with my friends when we go out.
3. She should ____________ for dinner.
4. I feel like ____________ my kids the truth.
5. I'm sorry I'm late. I had to stop ____________ to my landlord and that took me some time.
6. I can't believe she refused ____________ at the same place as us.

7. She wears these shoes __________ on weekends.

8. I forgot __________ you what I learned.

9. Chris didn't mind __________ there alone for an hour.

4 Some sentences below are incorrect. Check the incorrect ones and correct them. Study the example.

1. Paula did nothing but to sleep all day long. ☑
   Paula did nothing but sleep all day long.
2. Could the president to say that in public? ☐
   ____
3. They were sad to confirm their choice. ☐
   ____
4. I'd rather to be at home tonight. ☐
   ____
5. The boys had better wear sneakers play soccer. ☐
   ____
6. Carol dislikes being on her own. ☐
   ____
7. I hate to being stuck in traffic jams. ☐
   ____
8. She was thinking about going to the movies. ☐
   ____

5 What form do we use after the words below? Write *G* for gerund and *I* for infinitive. Add *to* after *I* when necessary.

1. imagine: __________
2. Modals: __________
3. know how: __________
4. before: __________
5. in: __________
6. about: __________
7. keep: __________
8. avoid: __________
9. it is no use: __________
10. agree: __________
11. would rather: __________
12. the first: __________
13. except: __________
14. want: __________
15. consider: __________
16. tell + object: __________

Link 5

1 **Choose the right column for each adjective and write its comparative.**

bright – smart – expensive – hot – cheap – comfortable – clear – friendly – large
serious – smelly – tasteful – cool – strong – careful – difficult

Short Comparative	Long Comparative

2 **Study the information about Dennis, Julia, and Mitchell. Then write sentences comparing their height, weight, and age. Follow the example.**

	Height	Weight	Age
Dennis	5'11"	176 lb	20
Julia	5'	123 lb	35
Mitchell	5'7"	180 lb	16

1. Weight:
   Dennis is fatter than Julia, but Mitchell is the fattest.
2. Height:
   ____
3. Age:
   ____

3 **Choose the best form of the adjectives to complete the sentences below.**

1. I am sure that is *more stupid / the most stupid* way to die.
2. What was *better / the best* score you got on the tests?
3. I have been to *higher / the highest* building in São Paulo.
4. This has never been *dirtier / the dirtiest* before.
5. English might be *easier / the easiest* than any other language.

6. Allan was *taller / the tallest* kid in class.
7. What is *worse / the worst* thing that has happened to you?
8. That was probably *sadder / the saddest* day of his life.

4 **Choose an adjective from the box and use it in the appropriate form to complete the sentences given.**

expensive – lazy – hot – strong – pretty – bad – good – far – intelligent – courageous

1. That was ____________ pizza I have eaten in my life! It was disgusting!
2. George used to be ____________ than me when we were kids. He hated any physical activity.
3. I wish I could give you a __________________________ present, but I have little money on me.
4. You were supposed to be ____________ than anyone else here! Don't you work out?
5. Otto was much ___________________ than all of the other kids. He grabbed the snake and threw it back into the jungle!
6. I believe today is ____________ yesterday. It is probably around 40° Celsius!
7. Don't you think Mirian is ____________ girl in the group? I believe she could be a model.
8. If you study more, you'll certainly become ____________________.
9. I think that if you add some sugar, this will be ____________ to eat.
10. Is Belo Horizonte _________________ than Goiânia for you to go and meet me?

5 **Use *less* or *the least* to complete the sentences given.**

Observe that *less* is used in the same way as *more than* and *the least* is used as *the most*; the difference is *less* and *the least* are used to show inferiority.

1. I know this is ____________ interesting text you've read.
2. Have you seen anything ____________ disturbing?
3. It was ____________ important thing you could think of.
4. I want to eat at ____________ expensive restaurant in this neighborhood.
5. They prefer to go on a ____________ adventurous trip next year.
6. I wish you were ____________ pretentious. You are so snobbish!
7. Suzie is ____________ ignorant girl from that group. She reads a lot!
8. Cats are usually ____________ active than dogs.

Link 6

1 **Circle the Passive Voice verb form considering the verb *give* and the tenses.**

1. Present Simple – do given / is given / had given
2. Past Continuous – should given / were being given / have giving
3. Present Perfect – must have given / has been given / have gave
4. Simple Future – will giving / will gave / will be given
5. Simple Past – were given / has being gave / has gave
6. Conditional – would can given / would be given / would have should given
7. Past Perfect – had been given / have given / was giving

2 **Select the sentences that are correctly written in the Passive Voice form and identify the verb tense they are in.**

1. By reading the books, I am learning new things about chemistry. ☐

____

2. The students have seen the movie the teacher recommended. ☐

____

3. All my money is being taken away! ☐

____

4. The questions will be asked to the candidates very soon. ☐

____

5. Coffee is considered excellent for the heart. ☐

____

6. The documents are showing the steps of the process. ☐

____

3 **Rewrite the sentences below in the Passive Voice, including the author of the action.**

1. Sly would bring some souvenirs from France.

____

2. My parents were offering me extra money.

____

3. The author has written a new novel.

____

4. The coordinator greets the students every day.

5. Fabio was choosing different patterns.

6. Next Monday John will present a lecture about new careers.

4 **Omit the author of the action and rewrite these sentences in the Passive Voice.**

1. People speak English all over the world.

2. One can find kangaroos in Australia.

3. The public chose the best candidate during the election.

4. They were downloading the new app.

5. We should always tell the truth.

6. Astronauts considered the Earth to be the most beautiful thing.

5 **Rewrite the sentence: "The book was written by that young author" in the:**

1. Simple Future

2. Present Perfect

3. Past Perfect

4. Conditional

5. Past Continuous

Link 7

1 **Determine if the sentences below are Zero, First, Second, or Third Conditionals.**

1. If they found some money, they wouldn't give it back. ____________
2. Drink water if you feel thirsty. ____________
3. If they had given me an opportunity, I would have thanked them. ____________
4. People reply politely if you talk to them appropriately. ____________
5. If I could, I would do anything to solve the problem.____________
6. I will go home if it gets any colder. ____________
7. If they call me, warn them I am in a bad mood! ____________

2 **Now, write if the sentences in exercise 1 are *facts* or if they are *possible*, *improbable*, or *impossible* to happen.**

1. ____
2. ____
3. ____
4. ____
5. ____
6. ____
7. ____

3 **The sentences below should be in the Second Conditional. Underline the mistakes and rewrite them to match the Second Conditional form.**

1. If I had more money, I will give it to the poor.

   ____

2. I could send it immediately, if I know the address.

   ____

3. If I had seen the problem, I would point it out.

   ____

4. She will buy it if she could save some extra money.

   ____

5. If all the kids had arrived early, we would have no problems.

   ____

6. They could have come, if you invited them.

   ____

4 **Choose a verb from the box and use it correctly in the following sentences.**

win – have – go – meet – buy – drink – do

1. If they had waited, I am certain they ________________ the actor from the play.
2. If she passes, she ____________ a party with her friends to celebrate.
3. I don't know what I ____________ if I were you.
4. If she practices more, she ____________ certainly ____________ the competition.
5. Julian ____________ an umbrella if it rains in the evening.
6. I would have helped you if I ____________ more money and free time.
7. If she ____________ earlier, everyone will do the same.

5 **The following sentences are into the First Conditional. Rewrite them into the Second Conditional.**

1. If Claire complains, her mother will blame me.

   ____

2. He will confirm the result if you speak to him.

   ____

3. If Keith comes to Brazil, I'll take him to Rio de Janeiro.

   ____

4. It will mean a lot to me if you read this book.

   ____

5. If my students study more, they won't have such bad grades.

   ____

6. If he plans better, he will have no problems during the trip.

   ____

6 **Rewrite the sentences from exercise 5 in the Third Conditional.**

1. ____
2. ____
3. ____
4. ____
5. ____
6. ____

Link 8

1 Change the expressions below from Direct Speech to Reported Speech.

1. tomorrow: ____________________
2. this: ____________________
3. yesterday: ____________________
4. these: ____________________
5. today: ____________________
6. here: ____________________
7. now: ____________________
8. next week: ____________________

2 Match the columns.

Direct Speech

1. Present Simple
2. Present Perfect
3. Present Continuous
4. Imperative
5. Must
6. Future
7. Said
8. Said to

Reported Speech

- [ ] Conditional
- [ ] told
- [ ] Simple Past
- [ ] Past Perfect
- [ ] said
- [ ] Have to
- [ ] Infinitive
- [ ] Past Continuous

3 Rewrite the sentences using Reported Speech.

1. Jill said: "I never do what I want".
____
2. Kevin said to me: "You helped me when I needed it most."
____
3. Leila said to Phil: "I will ask you a question about my behavior."
____
4. Saul said to Alex: "Are you trying to meet my boss today or tomorrow?"
____
5. The teacher said: "Pay attention to what I say and don't talk."
____
6. The boys said to the nanny: "You must play with us tonight."
____

4 **What did people say?**

1. Nina told me she was going home by bus.

   Nina: ______________________________

2. My brothers asked me if I could help them with a project

   My brothers: ______________________________

3. Diana told me not to worry about time or money.

   Diana: ______________________________

4. The secretary said she would go on vacation the following weekend.

   The secretary: ______________________________

5. Ella asked me what I most liked about her.

   Ella: ______________________________

6. She said she wanted to know where she could have lunch.

   She: ______________________________

7. He told me they were trying to break the wall.

   He: ______________________________

8. My parents said they would visit my grandmother the following week.

   My parents: ______________________________

5 **Underline the sentences with Reported Speech and circle the ones in Direct Speech in this paragraph extracted from the book *The Canterville Ghost*, by Oscar Wilde.**

About ten minutes later, the bell rang for tea, and, as Virginia did not come down, Mrs. Otis sent up one of the footmen to tell her. After a little time he returned and said that he could not find Miss Virginia anywhere. As she was in the habit of going out to the garden every evening to get flowers for the dinner-table, Mrs. Otis was not at all alarmed at first, but when six o'clock struck, and Virginia did not appear, she became really agitated, and sent the boys out to look for her, while she herself and Mr. Otis searched every room in the house. At half-past six the boys came back and said that they could find no trace of their sister anywhere. [...] He then ordered his horse to be brought round, and, after insisting on his wife and the three boys sitting down to dinner, rode off down the Ascot road with a groom. He had hardly, however, gone a couple of miles, when he heard somebody galloping after him, and, looking round, saw the little Duke coming up on his pony, with his face very flushed, and no hat. "I'm awfully sorry, Mr. Otis," gasped out the boy [...].

Extracted from http://www.gutenberg.org/files/14522/14522-h/14522-h.htm (accessed on December 14, 2012)

LINK 1 Communication Bytes

A: Hi, Bob. How was the job interview?

B: I got the job, Andrea. In fact, I've just started.

A: Cool! How is it going?

B: Pretty well, so far. I like animals, you know. What about you? You've already started working, haven't you?

A: Yeah. I started two days ago.

B: How was it?

A: Not bad. There are just two kids aged five and six. They're fine.

B: Do they obey you?

A: Well, they really like listening to stories, so we have a kind of a deal...

B: I see. You only tell stories when they are nice, right?

A: Yes, kind of. It's working well, so far.

LINK 1 Linked Skills

Host: Well, Lana and Tom. Are you ready? Then let's start the last group of today's questions. Here is the first question - Where is the Taj Mahal located: a. Thailand, b. India, c. Vietnam?

Tom: The answer is B, India.

Host: The answer is ... correct! Second question - What is the biggest country in the world: a. Russia, b. China, or c. Brazil?

Lana: The answer is A, Russia.

Host: Correct. The answer is correct! Third question - What happened from 1939 to 1945: a. World War I, b. World War II, or c. the Korean War?

Lana: The answer is C, the Korean War.

Host: The answer is ... not correct! The correct answer is B, World War II.

Be careful, Lana. Here is question number four - Who designed the principal buildings of Brasilia in Brazil: a. Roberto Burle Marx , b. Oscar Niemeyer, or c. Lúcio Costa?

Tom: The answer is B, Oscar Niemeyer.

Host: Correct. The answer is correct. Now you are even. Let's go to the three last questions ...

LINK 3 Linked Skills

Hello. At the southern extremity of this planet lies an icy, windswept, and virtually uninhabitable landmass. Antarctica is the world's fifth largest continent: a bleak and freezing place almost entirely covered by ice and plunged into darkness for much of its long winter. The geographer, Marinus of Tyre, coined the name *Antarctica* in the second century A.D., but many civilizations from the Ancient Greeks onwards believed in the existence of a great undiscovered southern land, but it wasn't until the 1840s that humans laid eyes on the continent. Since the early years of the last century, Antarctica has provided the scene for some of the greatest triumphs and tragedies of human exploration, most famously the death of Robert Falcon Scott on his return from the South Pole in 1912. Almost fifty years later an international treaty has set aside the entire continent as a scientific reserve and protected it from territorial claims.

LINK 5 Linked Skills

We were there when you finally got to ride on a donkey; we were there when you puddled in the freezing waves; we were there when your shorts were short and your mullet long and curly; we were there when you sunbathed until the sun had gone and then partied until it returned; we were there when you swam towards the horizon; and when you stared up at those stars. Teletext Holidays, we were there then, and we're here now, with great deals, a brand new website, dedicated Freeview on channel 101, and mobile apps, so that you can enjoy the best holidays of your life: teletextholidays.co.uk

LINK 7 Communication Bytes

HR: Good morning. How can I help you?

D: I'd like to stay a few nights in Manaus in late June. I intend to go to Parintins for the festival from there. Could you make a reservation, please?

HR: Sure. Better do it now because you may not find any rooms later. How many nights?

D: Three, please. Can you make sure there's air conditioning in the room?

HR: No problem, sir. How would you like to pay?

D: I'll pay by credit card.

HR: OK, sir. I'll need your full name and credit card number.

D: Dennis Pekarna, credit card number 568749853121583. Just one more thing: do you mind checking the bus fares to Parintins?

HR: I'm sorry, sir. I don't have access to this kind of information. Anything else?

D: No, that's it. You can confirm my reservation.

HR: The reservation has been made. If you need anything else, or if you have other questions, you can call us at this number.

D: Thanks!

HR: My pleasure.

LINK 7 Linked Skills

Robert Darnton: Brazil's emergence as a major world player provokes questions about its national identity, some of them hostile, such as the one you said you encountered on your last trip to the US: How can you live in a country overrun with favelas and violence? How do you answer them?

Lilia Moritz Schwarcz: It is strange how nowadays Brazil has a new image coming from abroad. We used to be seen as "exotics"; a country of Capoeira (a Brazilian form of martial art), Candomblé (a syncretic African religion), *Carnaval*, and the "Mulatas." Now we continue to be viewed as exotic, but the exoticism has a new ingredient: violence [...]

RD: [...] When I visit Brazil, I like to think I am in a country that is coping successfully with its history of racism. Could Brazil evolve into a multi-nuanced mestizo society like the one imagined by the Brazilian sociologist Gilberto Freyre?

LMS: Let me first ask you Bob, do you think of Obama as a "black President"? [...]

RD: Ask any American, ask Obama himself, the answer will certainly be that he is black. [...].

LMS: In Brazil, you are what you describe yourself to be. Officially we have five different colors—black, white, yellow, indigenous, and *pardo* (meaning "brown," "brownish," or "gray-brown"), but in reality, as research has demonstrated, we have more than 130 colors. Brazilians like to describe their spectrum of colors as a rainbow and we also think that color is a flexible way of categorizing people. [...] Also, in Brazil, if a person gets rich, he gets whiter. I recently talked with a dentist in Minas Gerais. As he is becoming old, his hair has turned white, and he is very well recognized in his little town. He started smoking cigars, joined the local Rotary Club, and said to me: "When I was black my life was really difficult." So one can see how being white even nowadays is a powerful symbol. [...]

Glossary

A

aboard - a bordo
abolished - abolido
above - acima
abroad - no exterior
absorb - absorver
accomplish - realizar
accomplishment - realização
achieve - realizar, alcançar
adolescence - adolescência
adulthood - vida adulta
advance - avançar
advancement - avanço
adventurers - aventureiros
advertisement - anúncio
against - contra
agricultural development - desenvolvimento agrícola
aid - auxiliar
aircraft - aeronave
alike - parecido
allergies - alergias
allies - aliados
allowed - permitido
amount - quantidade
ancient - antigo
anomaly - anomalia
appearance - aparência
applicant - candidato
application form - formulário
apply for - candidatar-se
arose - surgiu
arrival - chegada
assault - assalto
assess - avaliar
assign - atribuir
assisting - auxiliando
assortment - sortimento
at once - de uma vez
atmospheric - atmosférico
attach - anexar
attire - vestuário
autonomy - autonomia
available - disponível

B

babysitting - trabalhar como babá
background - experiência
backpacker - mochileiro
bail - fiança
bake - assar
ban - proibir
baptized - batizado
battles - batalhas
bazaars - bazares
be held - acontecer
bear - suportar
beauty - beleza
belief - crença
bellhop - carregador de malas
beloved - amado(a)
benefits - benefícios
beverage - bebida
blades - lâminas
blend - misturar
blow - soprar
bonfire - fogueira
boulders - pedregulhos
bridges - pontes
brownish - acastanhado
budget - orçamento
buildings - edifícios
built up - construiu-se
bullet - bala (munição)
bunking - estar alojado
burnt - queimado
business - negócio

C

caldron - caldeirão
calendar - calendário
captive - cativo
capture - capturar
carefree - despreocupado
caricaturing - caricaturando
carpenters - carpinteiros
cast off - livrar-se de
casually - casualmente
Catholicism - catolicismo
ceiling - teto
center stage - o centro do palco
chant - cântico
chapel - capela
chief - chefe
choice - escolha
Christian - cristão
church - igreja
claim - reivindicar
clerk - balconista
climb into - subir em
clusters - grupos
coal - carvão
coastal zones - zonas costeiras
cockpit - cabine do piloto
cocky - pretensioso
cologne - colônia
colonialism - colonialismo
colonies - colônias
coloring - colorir
commercialization - comercialização
commission - comissão
committed - comprometido
commonplace - comum
community - comunidade
complaint - reclamação
compliment - elogio
computer screen - tela do computador
concerted - combinado
connotation - conotação
conquer - conquistar
constructive - construtivo
contribute - contribuir
convenient - conveniente
cool - legal
cooler - refrigerador
cope with - lidar com
costumes - trajes
cottage - casa de campo
countless - incontável
craft - artesanato
critical - crítico
cruises - cruzeiros
cruising - cruzeiro
curly - encaracolado

current affairs - assuntos da atualidade
customer - cliente
customs - costumes
cutting - corte

D

dangerous - perigoso
dangling threads - fios pendurados
dawn - madrugada
decade - década
defensive - defensiva(o)
degree - graduação
deliverer driver - motorista de entregas
deluxe - de luxo
departure - partida
derail - descarrilhar
destination - destino
destructive - destrutivo
develop - desenvolver
dialectical - dialetal
dialects - dialetos
discovery - descoberta
dishes - pratos
disrupting - perturbando
distinguished - distinto
diving - mergulho
donkey - burro
downside - desvantagem
downtown - centro da cidade
drag - arrastar (pelo chão)
dramatic - dramático
drawbacks - inconvenientes
dress - vestir
drive shaft - eixo de transmissão
driver - motorista
drums - tambores
dubbed - apelidado
dune fields - dunas
duties - deveres
duty - obrigação
dynasty - dinastia

E

Earth - Terra
efficiency - eficiência
effort - esforço
emanate - emanar
emergence - emergência
employed - empregada(o)
employment - emprego
en route - a caminho
enclose - anexar
entrepreneur - empreendedor
equal - igual
equator - equador
escort - acompanhar
essential - essencial
estimated - estimado
evacuation - evacuação
evolve - desenvolver, evoluir
exotic - exótico
expeditions - expedições
expertise - perícia
exponentially - exponencialmente
exuberance - exuberância

F

facilities - instalações
fall under - cair sob
falling - queda
fares - tarifas
fast food counter - balcão de restaurante fast food
feasts - festas, banquetes
features - características
field - campo
fierce - feroz
fingernails - unhas
firecrackers - fogos de artifício de efeito sonoro
fireworks - fogos de artifício de efeito visual
firm - empresa
fish and chips shop - loja de peixe frito e fritas
fits - cabe, comporta
flatscreen - tela plana
flexible - flexível
flow - fluxo
folklore - folclore
form - forma
fraction - fração
free time - tempo livre
freedom - liberdade
freezing - congelante
frown on - desaprovar

G

gallop - galope
gastronomy - gastronomia
gathering - reunião
geared - orientada
geeks - nerds
glacier - geleira
glaciologist - glaciologista
glaciology - glaciologia
glitzy - chamativo
goal - objetivo
governance - governo
government panels - comitês do governo
ground - terreno
grown-ups - adultos
guardian - guardião
guests - convidados
gutted - eviscerado, vazio, oco

H

hairdresser - cabeleireiro
heat up - aquecer
heat - calor
heavy lifting - levantamento de peso
high school - colégio
hiking - caminhada
hire - contratar
hitching thumb - gesto para pedir carona
hold - possuir
hope - esperança
hospitality - hospitalidade

host - acolher, sediar
hostel - albergue
hostile - hostil
hotspot - ponto crítico
households - famílias
housekeeping cleaner - responsável pela limpeza
hunting - caça
husband - marido

I

ice sheet - manto de gelo
ice shelf - geleira
ice-free - sem gelo
identity - identidade
illegal - ilegal
illustrate - ilustrar
impose - impor
imprint - marca
incoming - recém-chegado
increased - aumentado
industry - indústria
inevitably - inevitavelmente
inflict - infligir
informal - informal
inherit - herdar
injuries - lesões
inspection - inspeção
instead - em vez de
insurance - seguro
interfere - interferir
interview - entrevista
intricacies - complexidades
intricate - intricado
intriguing - intrigante
Islamic religion - religião islâmica
itineraries - itinerários

J

job - trabalho
journey - jornada
joyful - alegre
jumbo jet - Jumbo

K

kayaking - caiaque
khakis - calças caqui
kick back - relaxar
kinetic energy - energia cinética

L

labor - trabalho
lakes - lagos
land - terra, pousar
late - tarde
laundry - lavanderia
law - lei
leftovers - sobras
license - licença
lift - levantar
linen - linho
lively - animado
logo - logotipo
loose gravel - cascalho solto
lucky - sortudo
luggage - bagagem
luxury - luxo

M

maids - empregadas domésticas
mainstream - corrente principal
maintained - mantida
maitre d' - chefe dos garçons
major - principal
manage - conseguir
marketplaces - mercados
martial art - arte marcial
masks - máscaras
masses - massas
matches - combina, partidas
mature - maduro
mayhem - celeuma, caos, desordem
meat - carne
melt - derreter
member - membro
mestizo - mestiço
method - método
Middle Ages - Idade Média
migrations - migrações
military - militar
mills - moinhos
mining - mineração
minors - menores
monitor - monitor
moon - lua
motion - movimento
moving traffic violation - infração de trânsito
multi-nuanced - multi-variada
Muslims - muçulmanos

N

nearly - quase, aproximadamente
neat - organizado
networking - trabalho em rede
nod - acenar com a cabeça
nomadic trade - comércio nômade
nomads - nômades
non-suit-wearing - uso de terno não obrigatório

O

oases - oásis
obscure - obscurecer, obscuro
obtain - obter
odors - odores
offend - ofender
offender - ofensor
offense - ofensa
offenseless - sem ofensa
offensively - ofensivamente
oil leaks - vazamentos de óleo
old fashioned - antiquado
on the fly - de improviso, de última hora
onboard - a bordo
once upon a time - era uma vez
ordinary - comum
otherwise - caso contrário

outdated - desatualizado
outdoors - ao ar livre
outside - fora
outstanding - marcante
overpriced - superfaturada(o)
overrun - invadir
ox - boi

P

packaging - acondicionamento, embalagem
pagan - pagão
paperwork - papelada
paraders - desfilantes
parent - pai ou mãe
parking - estacionamento
part-time jobs - empregos de meio período
patience - paciência
patrons - patronos
pattern - padrão
pebbles - seixos
penalties - penalidades
perfume - perfume
perhaps - talvez
permit - permitir
personnel - pessoal
physicist - físico
plains - planícies
plantations - plantações
plenty - abundância, muito
pocket - bolso
point out - assinalar, indicar
polar caps - calotas polares
police chief - chefe de polícia
pork - carne de porco
port - porto
power plant - usina
praise - elogiar
pregnant - grávida
pressed pants - calças com vinco
priest - padre
prime - primeiro, privilegiado
primitive - primitivo
prizes - prêmios
productive - produtivo
property - propriedade
provide - fornecer
provoke - provocar
publicly - publicamente
puddle - poça de água
purposes - fins, propósitos
pursuing - perseguindo

Q

quite - completamente
quotes - citações

R

racial slur - injúria racial
rafts - jangadas
rainbow - arco-íris
rainfall - chuva
raise - aumentar
rates - taxas
recall - recordar
recognized - reconhecido
reconnaissance - reconhecimento
reference - referência
registration - registro
regular fuel - combustível regular
reliable - confiável
remained - permaneceu
removal - remoção
renewable - renovável
replenish - reabastecer
requirements - requisitos
researchers - pesquisadores
responsible - responsável
restock - reabastecer
résumé - currículo
reversed - revertido
rewarding - recompensador
ride - montar
rivers - rios
road map - mapa das estradas
rocks - rochas
rubber - borracha
runway - pista de pouso e decolagem
rushes - corre

S

safest - mais seguro
sail - velejar
sales manager - gerente de vendas
saloon - salão
sand - areia
scattered - disperso(a), espalhado(a)
scenery - cenário
schedules - horários
schooling - educação escolar
scrap - sucata
seabirds - aves marinhas
seals - focas
seasick - enjôo em viagem marítima
seasons - estações
seat belt - cinto de segurança
self-sustaining - auto-sustentável
Semitic language - língua semítica
sensitivities - sensibilidades
service clerk - funcionário
set of tools - conjunto de ferramentas
set - estabelecer
settled - estabelecido
shaft - poço, mina
shared - compartilhado
ships - navios
shocking - chocante
shorelines - costa, margens da praia
showers - chuveiros
significant - significativo
site - local
sizes - tamanhos
slave trade - comércio de escravos
slavery - escravidão
slaves - escravos

Glossary

smart - esperto
smell - cheiro
snow - neve
soaked - encharcado
solely - unicamente
sparingly - com moderação
speakers - alto-falantes
species - espécies
spectators - espectadores
spectrum - espectro
sponsors - patrocinadores
square - praça
squeeze - espremer
stalkery - assédio, perseguição
stamp - carimbo
standards - padrões
step back - afastar-se
stranger - desconhecido
strength - força
stretch out - alongar
stuffing - preenchendo
stunning - deslumbrante
success - êxito
sugar - açúcar
suite - suíte
summary - resumo
summer - verão
sunbathe - tomar sol
support - sustentar
surface layer - camada superficial
surface - superfície
surpluses - excedentes
survey - pesquisa
suspicions - suspeitas
syncretic - sincrética
system of life - sistema de vida

T

tables - tabelas, mesas
tags - etiquetas
tear - lágrima
teenagers - adolescentes
temples - templos
terrain - terreno
testified - testemunhou
thin - afinar
thinkers - pensadores
thinning - redução
thrilled - emocionado
throughout - todo
throw - jogar
tongue - língua
tool - ferramenta
tow - reboque
toward - para, em direção a
trade routes - rotas comerciais
trading - comércio
transition - transição
treks - caminhadas
trick out - enganar
Turkish - turco
two-piece matched suit - terno de duas peças combinando

U

uncanny - estranho
underlying - subjacente
uneven - desigual
unforgettable - inesquecível
unique - único
unknown - desconhecido
upper floor - piso superior

V

vacuum - aspirar
valleys - vales
van - van
variation - variação
vehicle - veículo
veins - veias
venue - local
vessel - navio
village - aldeia
violations - violações

W

waiter - garçom
wallet - carteira
wandering - errante
warming - aquecimento
wastebaskets - cestos de lixo
water sources - fontes de água
wax - cera
wear - vestir
well pressed - bem passadas
well-fitting - bem encaixadas, bem ajustadas
whales - baleias
whether - se
whisper - sussurro
widely - largamente
wild - selvagem
wildlife - animais selvagens
wind turbines - turbinas eólicas
wind - vento
windmill - moinho de vento
wonder - maravilha
wood - madeira
work environment - ambiente de trabalho
work force - força de trabalho
worldwide - mundialmente
worn - usado
worry - preocupar-se

Y

yard - quintal
yield - produzir
yoke - jugo, peso
youth - juventude

Irregular verbs

Infinitive	Simple Past	Past Participle	Translation
be	was / were	been	ser/estar
become	became	become	tornar-se
begin	began	begun	começar
bet	bet	bet	apostar
bite	bit	bitten	morder
break	broke	broken	quebrar
bring	brought	brought	comprar
build	built	built	construir
burn	burnt / burned	burnt / burned	queimar
buy	bought	bought	comprar
catch	caught	caught	pegar
choose	chose	chosen	escolher
come	came	come	vir
cost	cost	cost	custar
cut	cut	cut	cortar
do	did	done	fazer
draw	drew	drawn	desenhar
drink	drank	drunk	beber
drive	drove	driven	dirigir
eat	ate	eaten	comer
fall	fell	fallen	cair
feed	fed	fed	alimentar
feel	felt	felt	sentir
fight	fought	fought	brigar
find	found	found	achar
fly	flew	flown	voar
forget	forgot	forgotten	esquecer
forgive	forgave	forgiven	perdoar
freeze	froze	frozen	congelar
get	got	gotten	obter
give	gave	given	dar

Irregular verbs

Infinitive	Simple Past	Past Participle	Translation
go	went	gone	ir
grow	grew	grown	crescer
have	had	had	ter
hear	heard	heard	ouvir
hide	hid	hidden	esconder
hit	hit	hit	bater
hold	held	held	segurar
hurt	hurt	hurt	machucar
keep	kept	kept	conservar
know	knew	known	saber
lay	laid	laid	colocar
lead	led	led	guiar / liderar
learn	learnt / learned	learnt / learned	aprender
leave	left	left	partir
lend	lent	lent	emprestar
let	let	let	deixar
lie	lay	lain	deitar
light	lit	lit	acender
lose	lost	lost	perder
make	made	made	fazer
mean	meant	meant	significar
meet	met	met	encontrar
pay	paid	paid	pagar
put	put	put	colocar
read	read	read	ler
ride	rode	ridden	conduzir
ring	rang	rung	tocar
rise	rose	risen	erguer-se
run	ran	run	correr
say	said	said	dizer
see	saw	seen	ver

Infinitive	Simple Past	Past Participle	Translation
seek	sought	sought	procurar
sell	sold	sold	vender
send	sent	sent	enviar
set	set	set	estabelecer
shake	shook	shaken	balançar
shine	shone	shone	brilhar
show	showed	shown	mostrar
shut	shut	shut	fechar
sing	sang	sung	cantar
sink	sank	sunk	afundar
sit	sat	sat	sentar-se
sleep	slept	slept	dormir
speak	spoke	spoken	falar
spend	spent	spent	gastar
split	split	split	dividir
spread	spread	spread	espalhar
stand	stood	stood	ficar em pé
steal	stole	stolen	roubar
swear	swore	sworn	praguejar / jurar
sweep	swept	swept	varrer
swim	swam	swum	nadar
take	took	taken	levar
teach	taught	taught	ensinar
tear	tore	torn	rasgar
tell	told	told	dizer / contar
think	thought	thought	pensar
throw	threw	thrown	arremessar
understand	understood	understood	entender
wake	woke	woken	acordar
wear	wore	worn	usar / vestir
win	won	won	ganhar
write	wrote	written	escrever

References

BOOKS

Dictionary

Cambridge Essential English Dictionary, by Cambridge University Press, 2004.

Longman Dictionary of Contemporary English, Pearson Education do Brasil, 2009.

Practical English Usage, by Michael Swan, Oxford: Oxford University Press, 2005.

Grammar

Collins Cobuild Student's Grammar, by Dave Willis, Harper Collins (UK), 1995.

English Grammar In Use, by Raymond Murphy, Cambridge University Press - ELT, 2004.

Fundamentals of English, by Betty Scharampfer Azar, Pearson - ELT, 2003.

Pronunciation

Better English Pronunciation, by J. D. O'connor, Cambridge University Press - ELT, 1999.

Pronunciation Plus, by Martin Hewings, Cambridge University Press - ELT, 1998.

Reading

Teens and the Job Game: Prepare Today-Win It Tomorrow, by Beverly Slomka MSEd, iUniverse Star, 2011.

Discoveries: North Pole, South Pole (Discoveries (Harry Abrams)), by Bertrand Imbert, Harry N. Abrams, 1992.

Betweeen Two Poles, by Amyr Klink, Bloomsbury Publishing PLC, 1995.

The Sahara Desert Angel: Education & Nature Folktales 2, by Vickie A. Soman, iUniverse, 2010.

Traveling Abroad: How To Proceed & Succeed, by Steven R. Tweh, AuthorHouse, 2011.

Career Match: Connecting Who You Are with What You'll Love to Do, Shoya Zichy e Ann Bidou, AMACOM, 2007.

Off The Grid: Modern Homes + Alternative Energy, Lori Ryker, Gibbs Smith, 2005.

Viva o Boi-bumbá, de Rogerio Andrade Barbosa, Ediouro Publishing, 1999.

300 Unmissable Events and Festivals Around the World, by Whatsonwhen.com, Wiley; 1 edition, 2009.

Festivals Around the World (Discover Other Cultures), by Meryl Doney, Orchard/Watts Group, 2002.

MOVIES

Wake Up Sid (India, 2009)

A vida de um jovem mimado em Mumbai que é motivado a experimentar uma mudança em seu estilo de vida quando encontra uma mulher em uma festa, que o inspira a "acordar" para a vida.

Expedição Antártida (Scott of the Antarctic, Inglaterra, 1948)

A verdadeira história do explorador britânico Robert Falcon Scott e sua malfadada expedição para tentar ser o primeiro homem a descobrir o pólo sul.

Uma Verdade Inconveniente (An Inconvenient Truth, EUA, 2006)

Um documentário sobre a campanha de Al Gore para fazer a questão do aquecimento global um problema reconhecido em todo o mundo.

Windfall (EUA, 2010)

O filme expõe o lado escuro do desenvolvimento da energia eólica, quando os moradores de uma comunidade rural no norte do estado de Nova Iorque cidade decidem adotar atitudes ecológicas.

Antônia (Brasil, 2006)

Quatro amigas de infância formam o conjunto de hip-hop, enquanto lidam com a violência da região onde moram e o machismo dentro da cena musical.

Ó Paí, Ó (Brasil, 2007)

O filme mostra a vida dos moradores em um cortiço do Pelourinho em Salvador no último dia de carnaval.

Histórias Cruzadas (The Help, EUA, 2011)

Uma autora aspirante durante o movimento dos direitos civis da década de 1960 decide escrever um livro detalhando o ponto de vista das empregadas Afro-americanas sobre as famílias brancas para as quais trabalham.

SITES

Adverbs

http://ajaja.paradoxinc.org/Basic/Tenses/PresentPerfectAdverbs.html

Cognates and false cognates

http://www.sk.com.br/sk-fals.html

http://www.solinguainglesa.com.br/conteudo/falsos_cognatos1.php

http://www.infoescola.com/ingles/falsos-cognatos/

Collocation

http://esl.fis.edu/grammar/easy/colloc.htm

http://esl.about.com/od/engilshvocabulary/a/collocations.htm

http://elc.polyu.edu.hk/advdicts/collocation.htm

Comparative & Superlative

http://www.englishexperts.com.br/forum/comparative-x-superlative-explicacao-detalhada-t210.html

http://oxforddictionaries.com/words/comparative-and-superlative-adjectives

Conditionals
http://www.englishpage.com/conditional/conditionalintro.html

Dictionary
http://dictionary.sensagent.com/perks/en-en/

www.enchantedlearning.com/dictionarysubjects/astronomy.shtml

www.ldoceonline.com/

www.merriam-webster.com/

www.morewords.com/

www.thefreedictionary.com

http://en.wiktionary.org/wiki/every

www.yourdictionary.com/

Direct and Indirect Speech
http://www.e-grammar.org/reported-speech/

Games and exercises
http://a4esl.org/q/h/vm/raise-rise.html

www.bbc.co.uk/ (click on Learning English)

www.english-zone.com/verbs/raise.html

www.hsw.uol.com.br/quiz-list.htm

http://kids.discovery.com/games/pompeii/pompeii.html

http://languagearts.pppst.com/affixes.html

Gerund, Infinitive, & Participle
http://owl.english.purdue.edu/owl/resource/627/01/

Grammar
www.edufind.com/english/grammar/

www.ego4u.com/

www.englishclub.com/grammar/

http://learnenglish.britishcouncil.org/en/quick-grammar

http://learnenglish.britishcouncil.org/en/grammar-games

http://learnenglish.britishcouncil.org/en/vocabulary-games

Idioms
http://idioms.thefreedictionary.com

www.yourdictionary.com/idioms

Indefinites and indefinite compounds
http://www.grammar-quizzes.com/agr_someany.html

Modal verbs
http://esl.fis.edu/grammar/rules/modal.htm

Past Perfect
http://www.learnamericanenglishonline.com/Yellow%20Level/Y15%20Past%20Perfect.html

Passive Voice
http://www.bbc.co.uk/worldservice/learningenglish/grammar/learnit/learnitv65.shtml

Phrasal Verbs
http://usingenglish.com/quizzes/

Prefixes
www.english-for-students.com/Negative-Prefixes.html

www.kwiznet.com/p/takeQuiz.php?ChapterID=1174&CurriculumID=26

www.primaryresources.co.uk/english/PC_prefix2.htm

Present Perfect
http://www.learn4good.com/languages/evrd_grammar/presentp.htm

Prepositions
www.englishpage.com/prepositions/prepositions.html

http://grammar.ccc.commnet.edu/grammar/prepositions.htm

Pronunciation
www.teaching-esl-to-adults.com/english-past-tense-pronunciation.html

Question tags
http://www.englishgrammarsecrets.com/questionstags/menu.php

Relative pronouns and relative clauses
http://www.ego4u.com/en/cram-up/grammar/relative-clauses

Songs
www.lyricstime.com

Suffixes
http://dictionary.reference.com/browse/-ize?qsrc=2446

www.learnenglish.de/grammar/suffixtext.htm

www.sk.com.br/sk-morfo.html

www.usingenglish.com/glossary/suffix.html

Tests
http://www.learnenglish.de/englishtestspage.html

Verb tenses
http://www.perfect-english-grammar.com/verb-tenses.html

Writing
http://esl.about.com/ and search 'writing skills'

www.wikihow.com/Write-a-Formal-Email

MISCELLANEOUS

Business News and Financial Information

http://www.forbes.com

Virginia Tech - Career Services

http://www.career.vt.edu

Design

http://richworks.in

NASA

http://www.nasa.gov

Science And Technology News Magazine

http://www.newscientist.com/

Deserts of the World

www.desertusa.com

Sample Consumer Complaint Letter

http://www.usa.gov/topics/consumer/complaint/complaint-letter.shtml

MadSci Network

http://www.madsci.org/

Ice Stories from Scientists

http://icestories.exploratorium.edu/dispatches/

Wired Magazine

http://www.wired.com

US Energy Information

www.eia.gov

Take a virtual travel to Brazil

http://www.v-brazil.com/

Book reviews

http://www.nybooks.com/

The Huffington Post

www.huffingtonpost.com

Página do Governo Federal

www.brasil.gov.br

Black Women of Brazil

http://www.blackwomenofbrazil.com/

Index

Vocabulary Log